D1436067

WITHDRAWN

Presented
with the compliments of
Glaxo Laboratories Limited

To___GASTROENTEROLOGY UNIT_____

Mr. A. T. Loades, BA(Hons)
'The Poplars'
Newlands Hill
Golden Valley Riddings
By _____ Derby DE55 4ES _____
Tel: Ripley (0773) 743346

Glaxo

DISEASES OF THE COLON AND RECTUM

A guide to diagnosis

Gastroenterology
Volume 3

DISEASES OF THE COLON AND RECTUM

A guide to diagnosis

Gastroenterology
Volume 3

J.J. Misiewicz C.I. Bartram P.B. Cotton
A.S. Mee A.B. Price R.P.H. Thompson

Glaxo Glaxo
Laboratories
Limited

Produced and published by
Gower Medical Publishing London UK for
Glaxo Laboratories Limited Greenford Middlesex UK

Project Editor: David Bennett

Layout: Peter Wilder

Illustration: Pamela Corfield

ISBN 0 906923 95 - 6

The sponsorship of this book does not imply approval or otherwise of any
of the products of the sponsor by the authors or contributors.

Printed in Italy by L.E.G.O. Vicenza

Preface

The text and the illustrations contained in this book provide extensive visual documentation of the normal and abnormal anatomy, histology, radiology, etc., of the alimentary tract, with supporting text. This text and these illustrations were not intended to form a textbook of gastrointestinal disease and should not be used, or judged, as such. Instead, the notes and illustrations form a convenient aide mémoire to remind the reader of various aspects of normal and abnormal gastrointestinal function and anatomy.

Gastroenterology is progressing and developing rapidly, and technological advances in imaging techniques and in the methods used to display the lesions of the alimentary tract have played an important part in the advance of the subject. The physician and the surgeon have a duty to keep up to date in their areas and I hope that this atlas will aid this aim. Diagnostic procedures and methods are described and histopathological appearances are treated in some detail, reflecting the importance of histopathological evaluation in alimentary disease, for example, in the area of pre-cancerous conditions. It is hoped that the contents of this volume will serve as a useful revision course for those active in gastroenterology and that it will stimulate others to become involved in this very dynamic area of medicine.

It has been a great pleasure to join with my fellow editors in the production of this book, which I hope will prove useful to many of our colleagues.

J.J. Misiewicz
Department of Gastroenterology and Nutrition
Central Middlesex Hospital
London, England

Authors

J.J. Misiewicz
BSc, MB, FRCP
Consultant Physician and
Head of Department of Gastroenterology and Nutrition,
Central Middlesex Hospital, London, U.K.

C.I. Bartram
MB BS, MRCP, FRCR
Consultant Radiologist,
St. Mark's and St. Bartholomew's Hospitals, London, U.K.

P.B. Cotton
MD, FRCP
Consultant Physician,
The Middlesex Hospital, London, U.K.

A.S. Mee
MD, MRCP
Consultant Physician,
The Battle Hospital, Reading, U.K.

A.B. Price
MA, BM, BCh, MRCPath
Consultant Pathologist,
Northwick Park Hospital and C.R.C., Harrow, U.K.

R.P.H. Thompson
DM, FRCP
Consultant Physician,
St. Thomas' Hospital, London, U.K.

Contents

9. Colon II: Disease of the Colon

10. Colon III: Crohn's Disease

11. Colon IV: Ulcerative Colitis

12. Colorectal Cancer, Polyps and Vascular Malformations

9.
Colon II
Diseases of the Colon

Infectious Diarrhoea

In the general population, some of the commonest causes of bacterial diarrhoea are the pathogenic strains of *Shigella spp, Salmonella spp, Escherischia coli, Campylobacter spp* and *Clostridium spp*. In travellers diarrhoea a wider range of organisms, including viruses, has been implicated.

When a colitis is present, blood and mucus appear in the stool with faecal leucocytes. The specific agent is identified by appropriate stool culture, and occasionally a rectal biopsy to exclude ulcerative colitis, or Crohn's disease is indicated (Fig. 9.1). Many cases resolve spontaneously but in over one third the precise pathogen is never isolated.

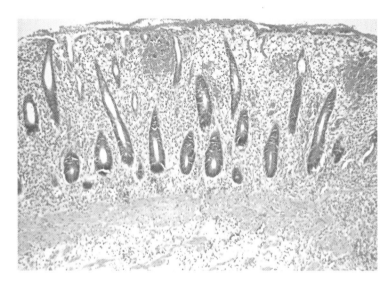

Fig. 9.1 Rectal biopsy in bacterial diarrhoea *(Campylobacter spp.)* showing marked mucosal oedema with polymorphonuclear leucocyte infiltration. Degeneration of individual crypt cells has given some crypts an attenuated appearance. H & E stain, × 30.

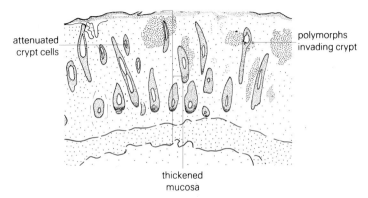

attenuated crypt cells

polymorphs invading crypt

thickened mucosa

Patients experience varying degrees of general malaise as well as diarrhoea and vomiting. It is now appreciated that homosexual men can also spread many pathogens via the anal route with disease usually limited to the rectal and anal regions.

Pseudomembranous Colitis

The formation of a 'pseudomembrane' on the colonic mucosa is a non-specific event which can arise in different types of colonic injury such as mercury poisoning, intestinal ischaemia, or in the course of severe infections, for example, bronchopneumonia. However, the commonest cause is antibiotic-associated colitis (Fig. 9.2). It has been shown that broad-spectrum antibiotics lead in some cases to colonisation of the large bowel by *Clostridium difficile*. The toxin produced by this organism is probably responsible for the syndrome. Patients with pseudomembranous colitis are pyrexial and have profuse diarrhoea,

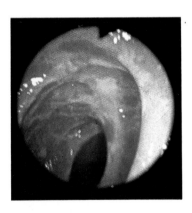

Fig. 9.2 Sigmoidoscopic view of pseudomembranous colitis due to antibiotic treatment. The yellow-white 'membrane' contrasts with the reddened colonic mucosa. Courtesy of Prof. R. Hunt.

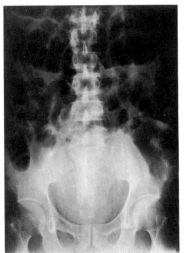

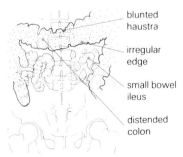

Fig. 9.3 Plain abdominal radiograph in pseudomembranous colitis.

blunted haustra

irregular edge

small bowel ileus

distended colon

abdominal cramps and tenderness. The diarrhoea usually does not contain blood or mucus, but this depends on the severity of the illness. In extreme cases, colonic perforation and toxic megacolon have been reported. Although most patients would have received broad-spectrum antibiotics (most typically clindamycin or ampicillin) at the time of illness, it is important to realise that in up to one-third of patients the treatment would have been stopped by the time symptoms develop.

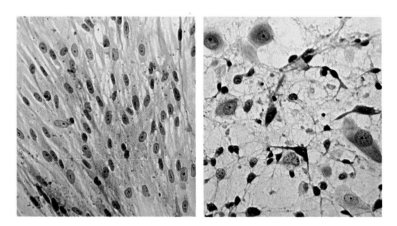

Fig. 9.4 Demonstration of the cytopathic action of *Clostridium difficile* toxin. The normal lung tissue growing on culture medium (left) has its fibroblasts regularly aligned, whereas the culture to which toxin has been added (right) shows gross disruption and marked nuclear changes.

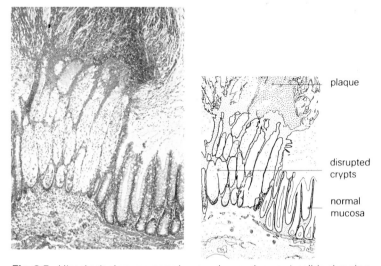

plaque

disrupted crypts

normal mucosa

Fig. 9.5 Histological appearance in pseudomembranous colitis showing the discrete nature of the crypt damage and almost 'volcanic' spray producing the plaque of fibrin, polymorphs and mucin debris. H & E stain, ×120.

The diagnosis rests on finding gross, or microscopic evidence of the characteristic pseudomembrane lining the colonic mucosa. This is most easily done by sigmoidoscopy and biopsy, although occasionally the pseudomembrane is present only proximally. Plain radiographs of the abdomen may show an irregular mucosal outline of the colon (Fig. 9.3). Barium enema appearances are often non-specific. The diagnosis is confirmed by culturing *Clostridium difficile* from the stools, or by showing the cytopathic effect of its heat-labile cytotoxin on cell culture (Fig. 9.4), an effect which is neutralised by antitoxin derived from a related species, *Clostridium sordellii*.

The biopsy in antibiotic-associated pseudomembranous colitis shows multiple discrete foci of disrupted crypts. The affected cluster of crypts is dilated and has shed the superficial half of the crypt lining into the lumen. This is seen as a spray of cellular debris, fibrin, mucus and inflammatory cells originating from the crypt surface and then forming the 'pseudomembrane' on the mucosal aspect (Fig. 9.5). Between such foci, the intervening mucosa is virtually normal (Fig. 9.6). The gross

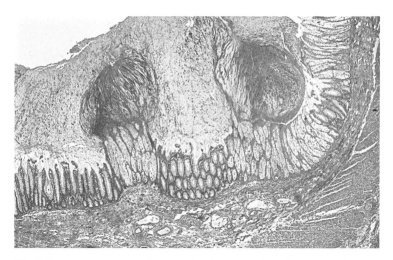

Fig. 9.6 Low power view of the section in the previous figure showing two discrete plaques separated by a zone of normal mucosa. H & E stain, × 30.

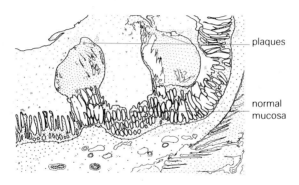

plaques

normal mucosa

specimen is unmistakable with the mucosal surface covered by a series of small yellow plaques (Fig. 9.7). In progressive disease the plaques coalesce to form a continuous necrotic membrane replacing the mucosa. The discrete lesions, rather than the more severe confluent picture, are diagnostic.

Amoebic Colitis

Amoebiasis is the result of infection with the organism *Entamoeba histolytica* (Fig. 9.8). Although the disease has a worldwide distribution, it is most prevalent in the tropics and in areas of poor sanitation. It may affect a number of organs, but the colon is usually the initial site. The organism exists in two forms: a motile trophozoite and a non-motile cystic form. The cysts are swallowed in contaminated water or food and change within the bowel lumen into the motile trophozoite form responsible for the clinical features of the illness. The cysts may become trophozoites at any time, but the factors responsible for this conversion are unknown. Most individuals who are cyst carriers remain asymptomatic. Thus patients harbouring amoebae can vary from asymptomatic to acutely ill with the colitic form of the disease. The cysts of *Entamoeba histolytica* must not be confused with the non-pathogenic *Entamoeba coli* (Fig. 9.9).

Amoebic colitis can resemble ulcerative colitis clinically with diarrhoea, preceded by cramping lower abdominal pain as the predominant symptom. The faeces are characteristically watery, but of small

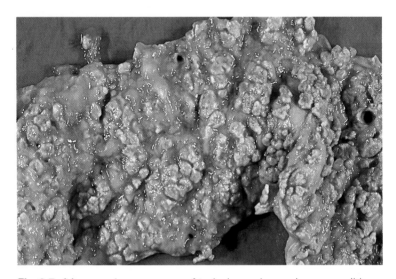

Fig. 9.7 Macrosopic appearance of typical pseudomembranous colitis showing the discrete yellow plaques.

volume and streaked with bloody mucus. This acute symptomatic phase may be fulminant, or continue for several weeks or even months, when it can be associated with marked weight loss.

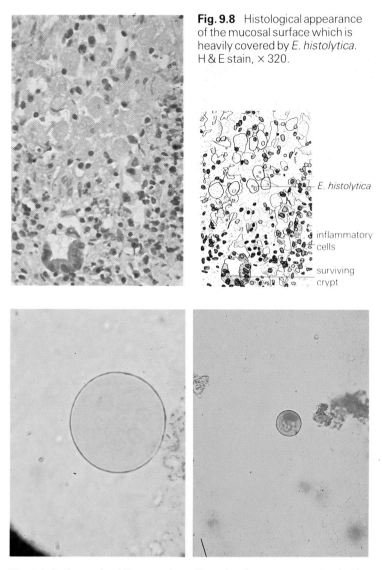

Fig. 9.8 Histological appearance of the mucosal surface which is heavily covered by *E. histolytica*. H & E stain, × 320.

E. histolytica

inflammatory cells

surviving crypt

Fig. 9.9 Iodine stain of *Entamoeba coli* cyst in a faeces preparation (left) and *E. histolytica* cyst (right) at the same magnification. Courtesy of Dr. D. Seal.

Sigmoidoscopy in the acute phase of the illness shows mucosal ulceration in 85% of patients (Fig. 9.10). The ulcers are typically rounded, or 'punched out', in appearance and surrounded by a narrow rim of hyperaemia and oedema with relatively normal-looking intervening rectal mucosa (Fig. 9.11). Up to 20% of patients have diffuse ulceration with an abnormal background mucosa. Scrapings from the ulcer base, blood-stained exudate, or liquid faeces (in order of

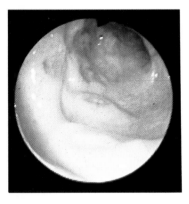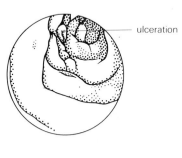

Fig. 9.10 Sigmoidoscopic view in amoebic colitis showing mucosal ulceration. Courtesy of Dr. C. Williams.

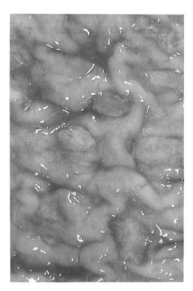

Fig. 9.11 Macroscopic appearance of the colonic surface showing amoebic ulcers. Courtesy of Dr. S. Lucas.

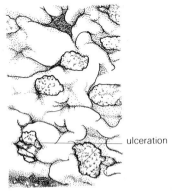

preference) should be obtained at sigmoidoscopy to show the presence of trophozoites and confirm the clinical diagnosis (Fig. 9.12). Amoebae can also be shown on the surface of a rectal mucosal biopsy, but this test is less reliable. Serological tests, including the indirect haemagglutination test and the amoebic complement fixation test, may distinguish patients with invasive amoebiasis from non-specific inflammatory bowel disease in difficult cases.

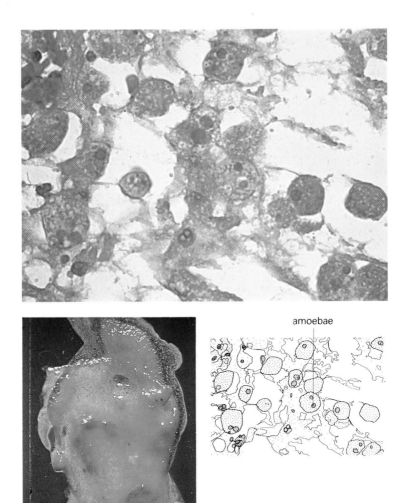

Fig. 9.12 Appearance of blood and mucus-containing stool in amoebiasis (above) and amoebae in stool smear (left), H & E stain, × 480). Courtesy of Dr. S. Lucas.

The radiographic features of amoebic colitis are varied and non-specific, ranging from discrete ulceration to toxic megacolon. Amoebic colitis may present with a diffuse granular colitis, indistinguishable from ulcerative colitis in 10–15% of cases, or deep shaggy ulceration similar to that seen in Crohn's disease or tuberculosis. Strictures may develop in chronic cases, and a typical appearance is a conical caecum with an irregular mucosal surface (Fig. 9.13). Amoebomas develop in less than 10% of patients. These are large ulcerated granulomatous masses found mainly at the flexures, in the caecum and rectosigmoid area (Fig.

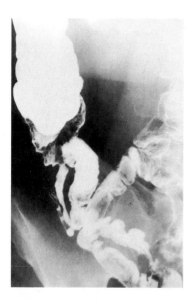

Fig. 9.13 Barium enema radiograph in chronic amoebic colitis showing a funnel-shaped caecum with granular deformity.

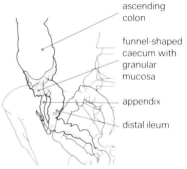

ascending colon

funnel-shaped caecum with granular mucosa

appendix

distal ileum

Fig. 9.14 Barium enema showing an amoeboma in the ascending colon.

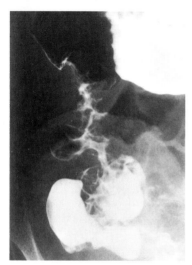

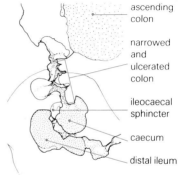

ascending colon

narrowed and ulcerated colon

ileocaecal sphincter

caecum

distal ileum

9.14). They can be multiple and indistinguishable from a carcinoma, but respond rapidly to anti-amoebic therapy.

The caecum and the rectum are the commonest sites of ulceration. The initial lesions are small, yellowish, mucosal elevations, which ulcerate to give the typical ulcers with overhanging edges, usually aligned in the transverse axis of the bowel. In severe disease large areas of mucosa can be lost, exposing the submucosa and muscle (Fig. 9.15). The amoebae are best stained with the Periodic-Schiff reagent (PAS) and are usually found close to the surface, or just beneath the

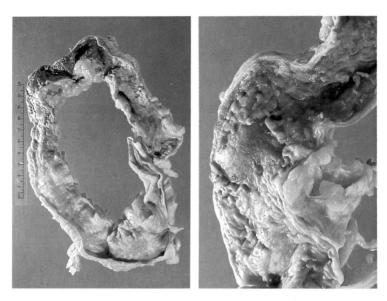

Fig. 9.15 Macroscopic appearances of the colon in a fatal case of amoebiasis. Most of the mucosa on the right side has been lost; some mucosa survives on the left side which is extensively ulcerated (left). A close-up view of the splenic flexure (right) also shows the extensive ulceration and some surviving mucosa.

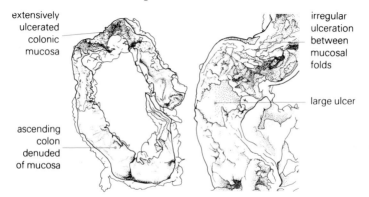

extensively ulcerated colonic mucosa

ascending colon denuded of mucosa

irregular ulceration between mucosal folds

large ulcer

overhanging mucosal edge. However, they may reside in the debris over the ulcer and it is important to process all tissue fragments received with a biopsy (Fig. 9.16). In sections they are often seen having engulfed red blood cells (Fig. 9.17) and this feature distinguishes them from the non-pathogenic *Entamoeba coli*. An inflammatory infiltrate is present in the ulcer floor and in the adjacent intact mucosa. Without finding the organisms however, the picture is not characteristic enough for a diagnosis to be made.

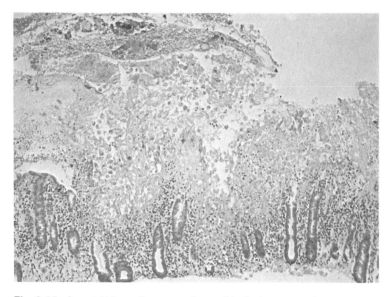

Fig. 9.16 A rectal biopsy in a case of amoebiasis demonstrating some invasion of the mucosa and also many organisms in the surface debris (left, H & E stain, × 75). This debris should be examined carefully as it may be the only site at which organisms are found.

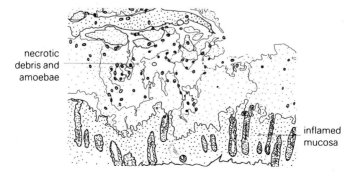

necrotic debris and amoebae

inflamed mucosa

Apart from complications such as perforation and spread to the skin, a state of post-dysenteric colitis can develop. This is persistent colitis and irritability of the bowel following an attack of amoebiasis. At this stage organisms are no longer detectable and it may be difficult to distinguish this syndrome from true ulcerative colitis that can occasionally arise, seemingly precipitated by an initial attack of infection.

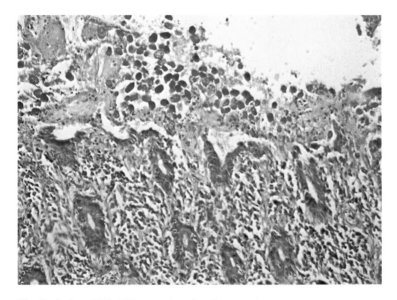

The Periodic-acid Schiff reagent stains the amoebae magenta (right, × 180) and is the best stain for detecting small numbers of organisms.

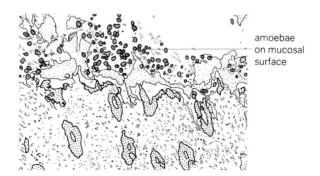

amoebae on mucosal surface

Amoebiasis is not confined to the intestinal tract and may affect a number of other sites, most frequently the liver, resulting in the formation of an amoebic abscess; pericarditis and meningitis also occur.

Pneumatosis Cystoides Intestinalis
In this uncommon disorder numerous gas-filled cysts are formed within the submucosa and subserosa of the large and small intestine. The

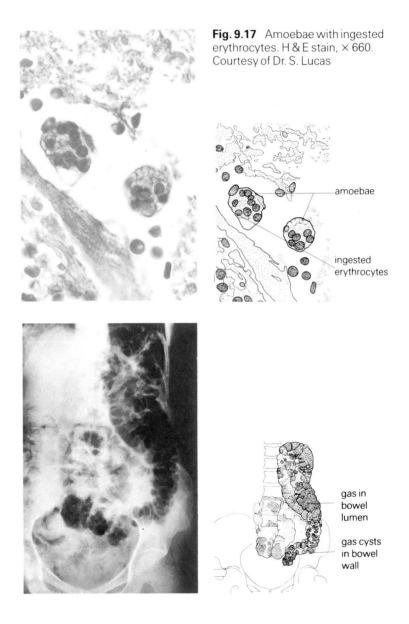

Fig. 9.17 Amoebae with ingested erythrocytes. H & E stain, × 660. Courtesy of Dr. S. Lucas

amoebae

ingested erythrocytes

gas in bowel lumen

gas cysts in bowel wall

cause is unknown, although there is an association with pyloric obstruction and with chronic obstructive airways disease. The composition of the gas within the cysts approximates to that of atmospheric air. It has been suggested that in patients with chronic obstructive airways disease gas may track down from the subpleural spaces retroperitoneally along the mesenteric vascular tree to the bowel wall. Pneumatosis cystoides may be an incidental finding on a plain abdominal radiograph (Fig. 9.18). Symptoms caused by the cysts include crampy lower abdominal discomfort, tenesmus, diarrhoea, rectal bleeding and profuse mucoid discharge. Intestinal obstruction, or a pneumoperitoneum from a ruptured cyst occur rarely.

Cysts can be seen at sigmoidoscopy (Fig. 9.19), or on barium enema, where they have the appearance of numerous round, filling defects (Fig. 9.20).

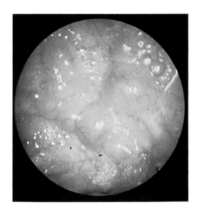

Fig. 9.19 Sigmoidoscopic appearance of submucosal gas cysts in pneumatosis coli.

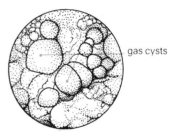

gas cysts

Fig. 9.20 Barium enema in pneumatosis coli showing the gas cysts in the bowel wall.

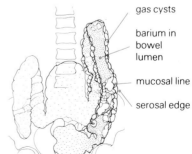

gas cysts

barium in bowel lumen

mucosal line

serosal edge

The pathological picture of pneumatosis is similar in the presence, or absence of co-existing disease (chronic airways disease, pyloric obstruction). If secondary, the cysts predominate on the serosa, but if idiopathic, they are found mainly in the submucosa. Macroscopically, the bowel has a spongy texture and mucosal blebs may be seen (Fig. 9.21 & 9.22). Polypoid cysts are rarely present and disappear when punctured.

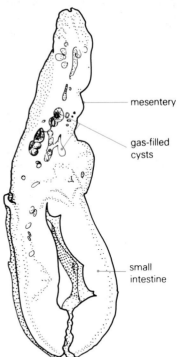

Fig. 9.21 Macroscopic appearance of cysts in pneumatosis intestinalis.

mesentery

gas-filled cysts

small intestine

Microscopy of the cysts reveals spaces lined in part by giant cells, in part by inflammatory cells and occasionally flat endothelial-like cells (Fig. 9.23). The pathogenesis of the cysts is not clear, but the presence of endothelial-like cells has been cited as evidence for an origin in distended lymphatics.

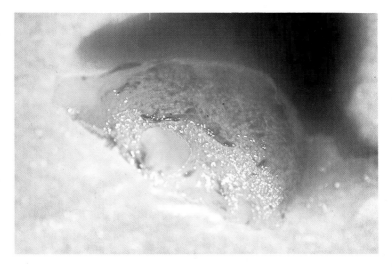

Fig. 9.22 Rectal biopsy in pneumatosis intestinalis showing a gas-filled cyst in the submucosa.

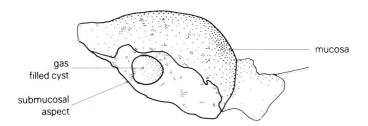

Actinomycosis

This is a rare condition due to infection with the fungus *Actinomyces israeli,* which is normally resident in the mouth. The ileocaecal region is most commonly infected following appendiceal rupture and the escape of actinomyces to form an inflammatory mass. The rectum is rarely involved, with stricture and fistula formation. Characteristically there is chronic inflammatory induration and sinus formation with extreme necrosis and fibrosis. Peritonitis is rare.

On microscopy of an actinomycitic lesion the colonies comprise a tangled mass of hyphae (mycelium) with peripherally arranged club-shaped bodies (Fig. 9.24). Within the gut wall the organisms must be associated with an inflammatory reaction before they can be considered pathogenic.

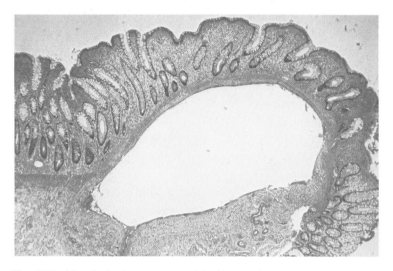

Fig. 9.23 Histological appearance of the biopsy shown in the previous figure, intact mucosa overlays the cyst which is lined by giant cells. (Individual giant cells are not visible at this magnification). H & E stain, × 75.

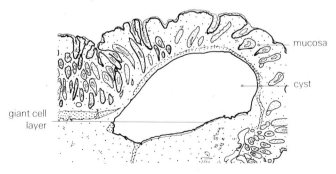

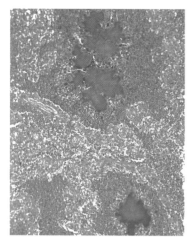 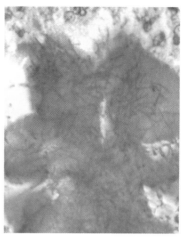

Fig. 9.24 Histology in actinomycosis; basophilic clusters of hyphae surrounding the appendix (not shown) (left H & E stain, × 20);

Periodic-acid Schiff reagent staining the actinomycetes magenta, hyphae are just visible at the margins of the colony (right, × 180).

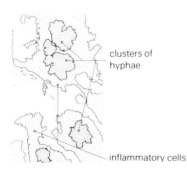

clusters of hyphae

inflammatory cells

hyphal mass

strands of hyphae

With the Gomori-Grocott stain the hyphae appear black (left, × 320).

hyphae

Pseudomyxoma Peritonei

This is an uncommon disorder in which the peritoneal cavity becomes filled with mucinous material which may be present either as numerous cystic masses, or lying freely within the abdominal cavity. It may be due to rupture of a benign lesion such as a mucocoele of the appendix (Fig. 9.25), or an ovarian cystadenoma. Alternatively, the condition may be part of a neoplastic process such as a mucus-producing adenocarcinoma, most commonly affecting the ovary, but also the bowel, urachal cysts or the common bile duct. It is difficult on histological grounds to forecast whether the behaviour will be benign or malignant. A range of appearances includes simple mucinous debris, mucin and numbers of bland mucus-producing epithelial cells, or obvious malignant mucus-producing epithelium (Fig. 9.26). Because recurrence and spread can occur with benign histological appearances it is argued that the disorder is never benign, but represents spread from a highly differentiated carcinoma.

Melanosis Coli

Melanosis coli is a benign condition found in people who habitually use anthracene-containing laxatives. It is characterised by pigmentation of the colonic mucosa due to the accumulation of pigment-containing macrophages in the mucosa of the large bowel (Fig. 9.27). These are

Fig. 9.25 A mucocele of the appendix.

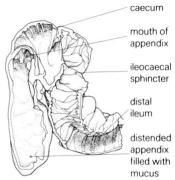

caecum

mouth of appendix

ileocaecal sphincter

distal ileum

distended appendix filled with mucus

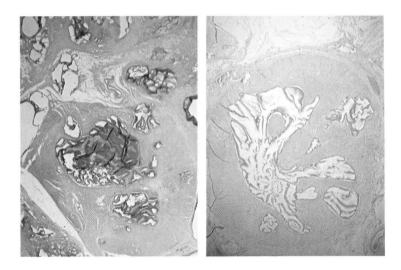

Fig. 9.26 Histological appearances of a mucin-secreting adenocarcinoma of the appendix which has penetrated the full thickness of its wall. Alcian Blue stain (left) and H & E stain (right). × 10.

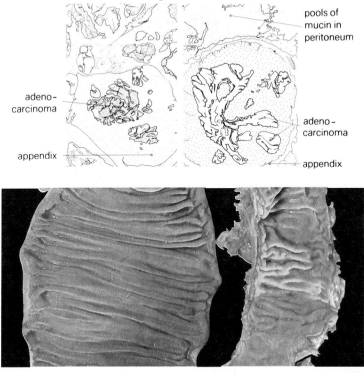

Fig. 9.27 Deeply pigmented colonic mucosa in melanosis coli compared with the normal mucosal colour.

easily seen histologically (Fig. 9.28). The pigment is not true melanin but more akin to the group of pigments known as lipofuscins. When gross, the condition may be recognised sigmoidoscopically as brownish-black areas (Fig. 9.29) and confirmed on rectal biopsy. The presence of pigmentation is not harmful and is reversible on discontinuing the laxative.

Appendicitis
Acute inflammation of the appendix is the commonest cause of emergency abdominal surgery in the West. Approximately 5 to 7%

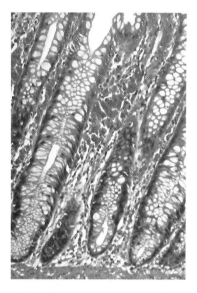

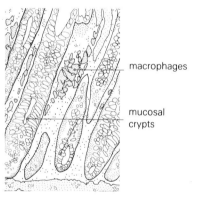

Fig. 9.28 Histological appearance in melanosis coli showing pigment-laden macrophages between the crypts in the lamina propria. H & E stain, × 120.

macrophages

mucosal crypts

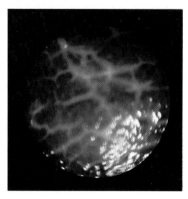

Fig. 9.29 Sigmoidoscopic appearance of submucosal pigmentation in melanosis coli.

of people develop appendicitis at some time during their lives. The condition is commonest in the second and third decades of life and is uncommon in children below the age of five or in the elderly.

The precise cause of appendicitis is unknown, but it is thought to be due to obstruction of the appendiceal lumen, most often by a faecolith. This results in bacterial proliferation and invasion of the hypoxic mucosal lining of the appendix. As faecoliths are more common with a diet low in fibre, it has been suggested that acute appendicitis can be added to the list of dietary fibre deficiency diseases. Rarely, a carcinoid tumour in the tip of the appendix may be the cause (Fig. 9.30).

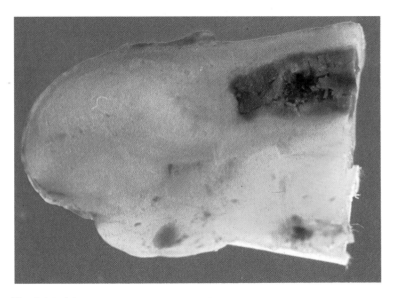

Fig. 9.30 Macroscopic appearance of a carcinoid tumour in the tip of the appendix.

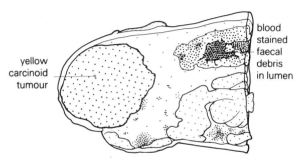

Acute appendicitis is classified as simple, gangrenous, or perforated on the basis of laparotomy and histological findings. Patients present with anorexia, nausea and abdominal pain, most commonly located in the right fossa. On examination they are usually pyrexial and there is tenderness and a guarding with rebound in the right iliac fossa. Laboratory investigations are mostly unhelpful, although leucocytosis is a frequent finding. Perforation can result in generalised peritonitis, or in a walled-off abscess which may either resolve spontaneously, or need

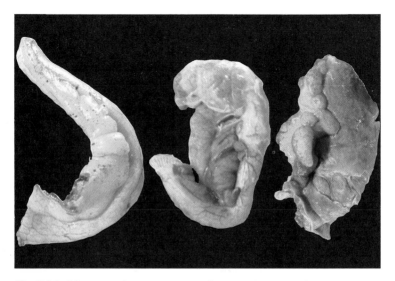

Fig. 9.31 Macroscopic appearances of a normal appendix (left) and increasing degrees of inflammation (middle and right).

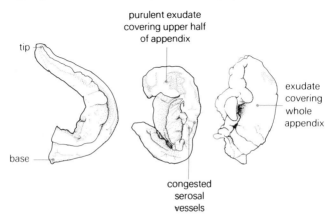

tip

purulent exudate covering upper half of appendix

exudate covering whole appendix

base

congested serosal vessels

surgical drainage. The earliest macroscopic abnormalities are congestion of the serosal vessels, followed by dilatation of the appendix which usually involves the tip. Subsequently it is the distal half that becomes swollen and covered by a purulent exudate (Figs. 9.31 & 9.32). The lumen also contains a purulent exudate, or a faecolith. At a later stage the tip and the rest of the organ may be soft, purplish, haemorrhagic and necrotic.

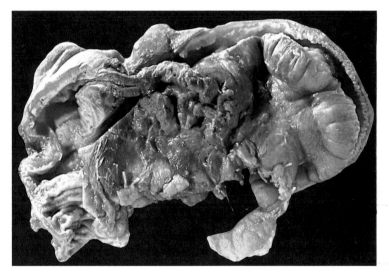

Fig. 9.32 Macroscopic appearances in acute appendicitis with a periappendiceal mass.

opened proximal half of appendix

caecum

ascending colon

ileum

distal half of appendix

haemorrhagic inflammatory mass surrounding distal appendix

Histology shows a progressively severe acute inflammatory infiltrate starting in the mucosa and spreading through the full thickness of the wall (Fig. 9.33). The severity will depend on the time at which surgery was performed.

Abdominal Tuberculosis
Tuberculous involvement of the intestine due to infection with either *Mycobacterium tuberculosis* or *Mycobacterium bovis* is now uncommon in the West, although it has been increasingly diagnosed in immigrants. It is still a major cause of non-neoplastic bowel disease in emergent countries. The condition may be either primary with no evidence of tuberculosis elsewhere in the body, or secondary, with the disease present in other organs, most commonly the lung.

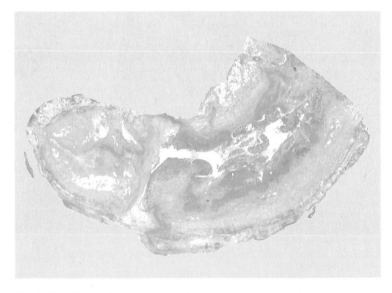

Fig. 9.33 Histological appearance in acute appendicitis showing a perforation close to the tip. The mucosa is ulcerated and a florid inflammatory infiltrate is present throughout the wall and on the peritoneal surface. H & E stain, × 12.

necrotic mucosa

appendiceal lumen

muscle coat

perforation

peritoneal inflammation

The ileocaecal region is most often affected (Fig. 9.34), although any part of the colon can be involved. The disease may take three forms: hypertrophic, which is more commonly a primary lesion and clinically benign; ulcerative, in which ulceration is predominant (Fig. 9.35) and ulcerohypertrophic, which combines the features of the other two.

The clinical features of abdominal tuberculosis are non-specific. Symptoms are usually chronic and include weight loss, cramping lower abdominal pain, diarrhoea and occasionally the passage of blood. The sedimentation rate is almost always raised. In the United Kingdom the disease is virtually confined to immigrants from the third world countries, in whom other non-infective inflammatory conditions of the bowel are rare. Abdominal tuberculosis should be suspected in these circumstances, particularly when pulmonary symptoms are present,

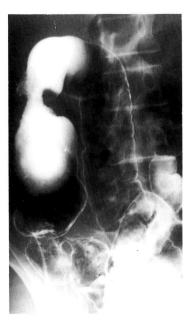

Fig. 9.34 Barium enema in ileocaecal tuberculosis showing the dilated ileum, patulous ileocaecal sphincter, contracted caecum and a short stricture in the ascending colon. Courtesy of Dr. H. H. Shawdon.

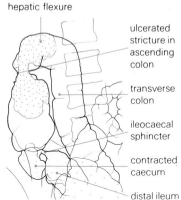

hepatic flexure

ulcerated stricture in ascending colon

transverse colon

ileocaecal sphincter

contracted caecum

distal ileum

although this is uncommon. Complications of ileocaecal tuberculosis, such as obstruction, malabsorption due to a stricture (Fig. 9.36), deep ulceration, fistulisation, or perforation, are infrequent.

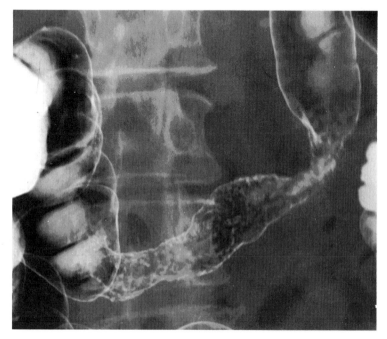

Fig. 9.35 Barium enema in tuberculous colitis showing a well demarcated stricture in the mid-transverse colon containing confluent superficial ulceration.

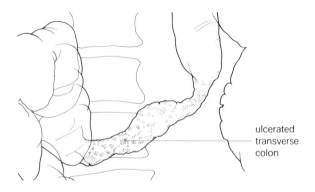

ulcerated transverse colon

Physical examination shows a mass in the right iliac fossa in most patients with ileocaecal tuberculosis. Ascites may be present if peritoneal involvement is prominent. It may be difficult to confirm the

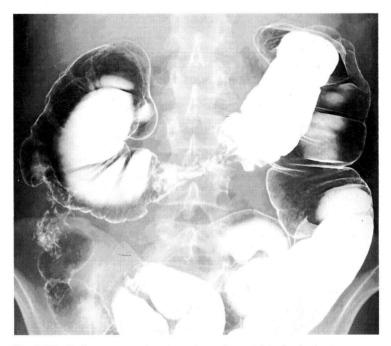

Fig. 9.36 Barium enema showing tuberculous stricturing in the transverse colon and ascending colon.

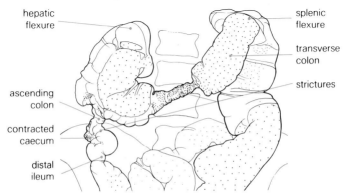

diagnosis and a suggestive chest radiograph (Fig. 9.37) or a positive Mantoux test (see 'Small Intestine II') are important clues. Radiological appearances are often non-specific and may be confused with other granulomatous diseases of the large bowel and ileocaecal region, including Crohn's disease and yersiniosis. Nevertheless, certain features are suggestive of tuberculous involvement. These include a circumferential plane to the ulceration (Fig. 9.38), annular strictures sharply demarcated from normal bowel (see Fig. 9.36), a conical contracted caecum with a patulous ileocaecal sphincter (see Fig. 9.34), deep shaggy ulceration (Fig. 9.39) and a hypertrophic mass (Fig. 9.40).

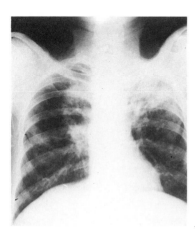

Fig. 9.37 Chest radiograph in active pulmonary tuberculosis showing apical infiltration and early cavitation.

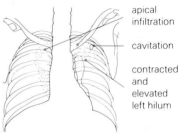

apical infiltration

cavitation

contracted and elevated left hilum

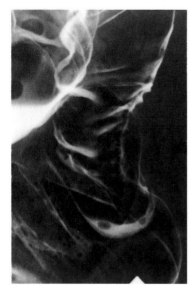

Fig. 9.38 Tuberculous transverse ulceration in the proximal descending colon.

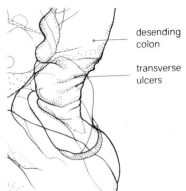

desending colon

transverse ulcers

In difficult cases a trial of anti-tuberculous therapy, laparotomy with full thickness biopsy of the affected bowel wall, or removal of a peritoneal tubercle may be necessary to confirm a clinical diagnosis.

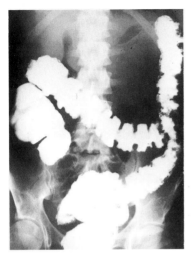

Fig. 9.39 Tuberculosis colitis with extensive deep shaggy ulcers.

ulceration

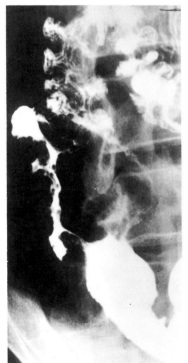

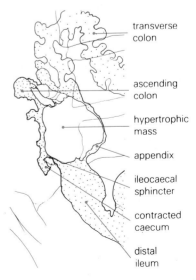

Fig. 9.40 Barium enema in hypertrophic TB, mainly affecting the ascending colon in a 32-year-old Indian presenting with a large mass in the right iliac fossa.

transverse colon

ascending colon

hypertrophic mass

appendix

ileocaecal sphincter

contracted caecum

distal ileum

The pathology of colonic tuberculosis is similar to that described in the 'Small Intestine II'. Single or multiple short strictures, or ulcerative lesions may be present. The ulcerative lesions are sharply defined with a surrounding thickened bowel wall. The cobblestone pattern seen in Crohn's disease, which usually involves a greater length of bowel, is not present (Fig. 9.41).

Histology shows confluent, usually caseating, giant-cell granulomas (Fig. 9.42). The muscle coat is frequently destroyed in TB (but spared in Crohn's disease) and fissuring ulceration is not seen. The presence of acid-fast tubercle bacilli demonstrated by the Ziehl-Neelsen stain confirms the diagnosis (Fig. 9.43).

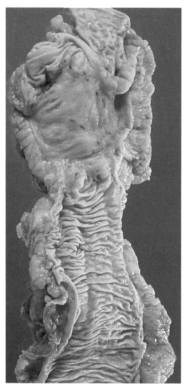

Fig. 9.41 Macroscopic appearance of·the ileocaecal region in intestinal tuberculosis, showing the thickened, flattened, featureless caecal mucosa and small haemorrhagic ulcers.

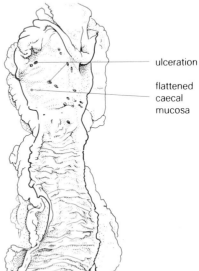

ulceration

flattened caecal mucosa

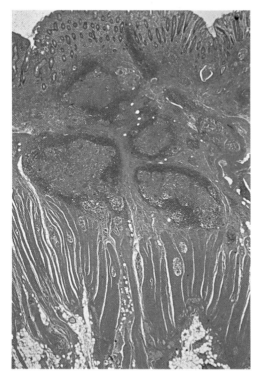

Fig. 9.42 Histological appearance in colonic TB showing large confluent granulomas in the submucosa and extending into the muscle wall. These granulomas are much larger than those seen in Crohn's colitis. H & E stain, × 12.

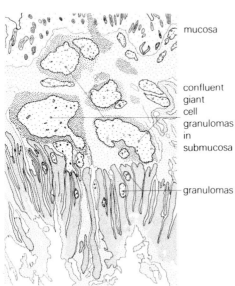

mucosa

confluent giant cell granulomas in submucosa

granulomas

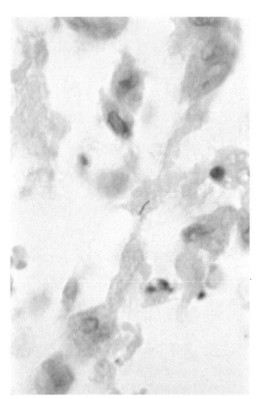

Fig. 9.43 A Ziehl-Neelsen stain showing an acid fast mucobacterium, × 1200.

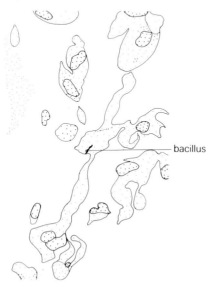

bacillus

10.
Colon III
Crohn's Disease

Introduction

Crohn's disease is a chronic inflammatory condition of unknown aetiology. It may affect any part of the gastrointestinal tract from mouth to anus, but most commonly it involves the ileocaecal region, small bowel, or colon. The disorder is mainly confined to the Western hemisphere and tends to affect young people in the second and third decades of life, although no age group is exempt. Crohn's disease and ulcerative colitis (see 'Colon IV') share the term 'inflammatory bowel disease' because they have many similarities. Nevertheless, in most patients a diagnosis of one or other of the two diseases can be made.

The aetiology and pathogenesis of Crohn's disease is unknown. A number of immunological phenomena have been described and recent work has suggested that an infective agent, possibly a small RNA virus or atypical mycobacterium, may be responsible.

The clinical picture varies with the site, extent and severity of the disease. The age of the patient is also important: children can have growth failure alone, occasionally without gastrointestinal symptoms (Fig. 10.1). Disease affecting the small bowel (Fig. 10.2) usually leads to diarrhoea without overt blood loss. Depending on the site and extent of the inflammatory process malabsorption may be present, including anaemia as a result of iron, folate, or vitamin B_{12} deficiencies, oedema due to hypoalbuminaemia and clubbing of the nails (Fig. 10.3). Pyrexia and weight loss are common. Narrowing of the bowel lumen by inflammatory oedema, or by a fibrous stricture leads to obstruction.

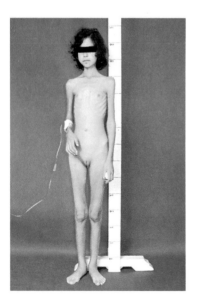

Fig. 10.1 Growth failure in a girl with Crohn's disease. This girl, aged 15, had a three month history of diarrhoea. Her height and weight are both below the 3rd percentile and secondary sexual characteristics are absent. Her bone age was only 10, indicating that the disease had been present for far longer than her symptoms suggest.

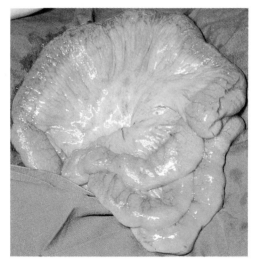

Fig. 10.2 Laparotomy in florid Crohn's disease of the mid-ileum showing a section of inflamed bowel, large mesenteric nodes and 'fat wrapping'. Courtesy of Mr. J. Alexander-Williams.

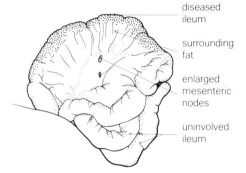

diseased ileum

surrounding fat

enlarged mesenteric nodes

uninvolved ileum

Fig. 10.3 Clubbing of the toes in Crohn's disease.

This may also occur with disease in the ileocaecal region which is the most commonly affected site (Fig. 10.4). A tender mass may be palpable in the right iliac fossa. Occasionally, patients initially present with abdominal symptoms mimicking appendicitis and an acute ileitis is found at laparotomy. It should be noted however, that another common cause of acute ileitis is yersiniosis and not Crohn's disease.

Colonic involvement (Fig. 10.5) is more likely to cause diarrhoea associated with overt blood loss, such as occurs in ulcerative colitis, but less severe malabsoption is absent. The common symptoms of Crohn's disease are summarised in Fig. 10.6. The anorectal region is the

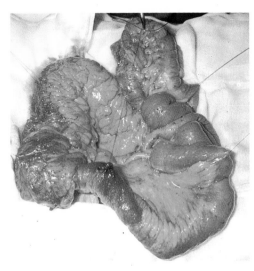

Fig. 10.4 Laparotomy appearance in Crohn's ileo-colitis, where a 'skip lesion' (normal bowel between diseased segments) and fistula may be seen. Involved bowel has a prominent fat wrapping. Courtesy of Mr. J. Alexander-Williams.

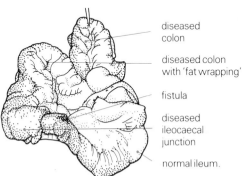

diseased colon

diseased colon with 'fat wrapping'

fistula

diseased ileocaecal junction

normal ileum.

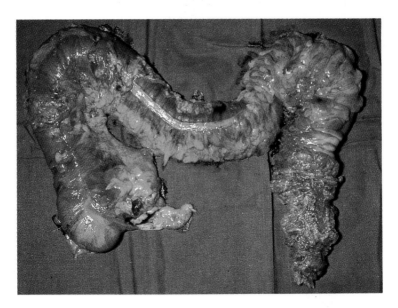

Fig. 10.5 Total colectomy for Crohn's colitis. The whole of the large intestine is involved by granulomatous colitis. Courtesy of Mr. J. Alexander-Williams.

Symptoms of Crohn's Disease	
Diarrhoea	70–90%
Rectal bleeding	45%
Abdominal pain	45–66%
Anal lesions	50–80%
Weight loss	65–75%
Fever	30–40%
Fistula	8–10%

Fig. 10.6 Common symptoms of Crohn's disease.

primary site of involvement in a minority of cases, although anal lesions are common in patients with active Crohn's disease elsewhere, especially when the colon is affected. Anal lesions include fissures,

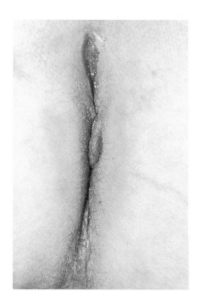

Fig. 10.7 Anal fistula in Crohn's disease.

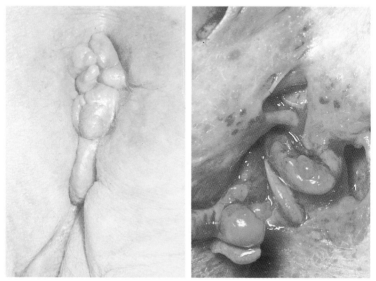

Fig. 10.8 Inflammatory oedematous tags without (left) and with (right) severe ulceration. Courtesy of Mr. J. P. S. Thomson.

fistulae (Fig. 10.7), inflammatory tags (Fig. 10.8) and protuberant tissue which may be mistaken for haemorrhoids. Gross inflammation and fistula formation are also found (Fig. 10.9).

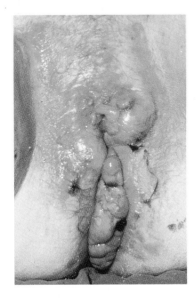

Fig. 10.9 Gross inflammation of the vulva extending from the anus in a young patient with Crohn's disease.

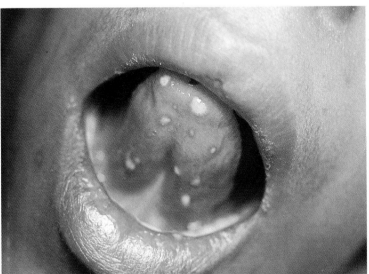

Fig. 10.10 Oral aphthous ulceration in Crohn's disease.

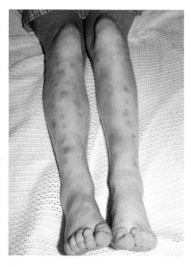

Fig. 10.11 Erythema nodosum. Courtesy of Dr. A. Bamji.

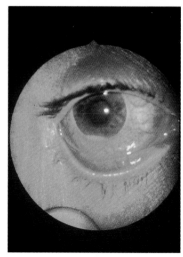

Fig. 10.12 Iritis. In this case there is considerable conjunctival injection and a hypopyon is also present. Courtesy of Dr. Ian Haslock.

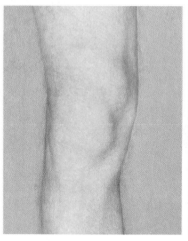

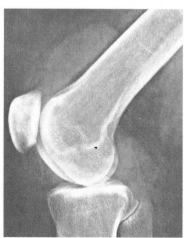

Fig. 10.13 Arthropathy of the knee showing an effusion arthropathy in the suprapatellar pouch. Courtesy of Dr. P. Dieppe.

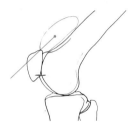

effusion in suprapatellar pouch

The course of the disease is unpredictable and there is a tendency to spontaneous remission and relapse. Active disease may be associated with a number of extra-intestinal lesions, such as oral aphthous ulceration (Fig. 10.10), erythema nodosum (Fig. 10.11), iritis (Fig. 10.12) or episcleritis and an arthropathy, which mainly affects the larger joints (Fig. 10.13). These features are thought to be related to the formation of circulating immune complexes. Another aspect cf skeletal involvement is sacroiliitis (Fig. 10.14), although unlike the arthropathy, it does not appear to depend on the activity of the disease.

A further feature of Crohn's disease (which does not occur in ulcerative colitis) is the presence of fistulae. These tend to result from continuing untreated active disease, or arise following surgery, particularly when operations are performed on patients with active inflammation. The fistulae can be either internal, between loops of bowel, bladder, or vagina, or they can open onto the skin, either on the

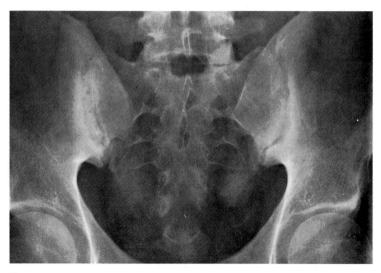

Fig. 10.14 Pelvic radiograph showing bilateral sacroilitis in Crohn's disease. The lumbar spine was normal and there was no evidence of ankylosing spondylitis.

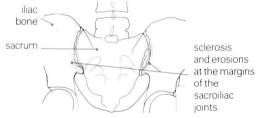

abdominal wall (Fig. 10.15) or around the anus. Surgery is usually necessary, although in some patients closure may follow appropriate medical therapy.

Other complications include cholesterol gallstones or oxalate renal stones. In patients with ileal disease a failure of the diseased segment to reabsorb bile salts results in the formation of lithogenic bile, leading to cholesterol gallstones. Oxalate renal stones are caused by the preferential complexing of calcium with malabsorbed fatty acids in the lumen on the small intestine, leaving free oxalates to be absorbed by the colon (Fig. 10.16).

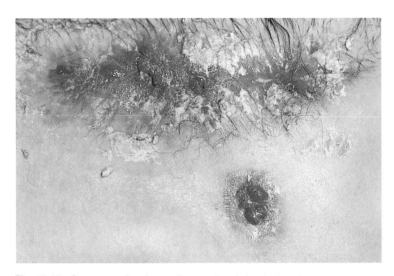

Fig. 10.15 Cutaneous fistulae on the anterior abdominal wall.

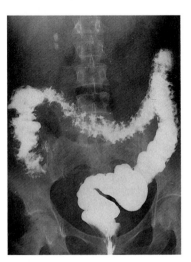

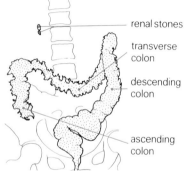

Fig. 10.16 Barium enema in extensive Crohn's colitis with two right renal calculi.

renal stones

transverse colon

descending colon

ascending colon

Investigation of a patient suspected of having Crohn's disease should include sigmoidoscopy and rectal biopsy. The sigmoidoscopic appearance in Crohn's disease is frequently normal, particularly when there is no colonic involvement. However, even then, there may be histopathological changes suggesting the diagnosis (see below). Sigmoidoscopy may show the presence of small aphthous ulcers with a normal intervening mucosa (Fig. 10.17), or more diffuse inflammatory change similar to that seen in ulcerative colitis including granularity, contact bleeding and ulceration. In difficult cases visualisation of more proximal segments of bowel may be necessary, when colonoscopic features include shallow linear ulcers (Fig. 10.18) and a 'cobblestone' appearance due to submucosal oedema (Fig. 10.19).

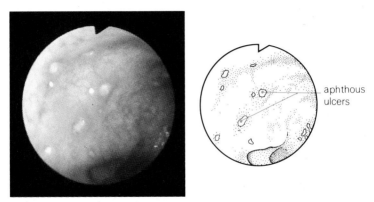

aphthous ulcers

Fig. 10.17 Colonoscopic appearance of aphthous ulceration. Courtesy of Dr. D. P. Jewell.

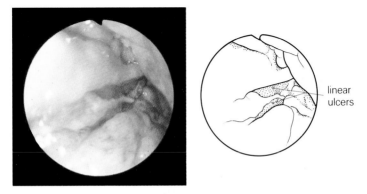

linear ulcers

Fig. 10.18 Colonoscopic appearance of linear ulceration.

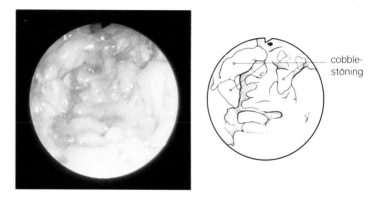

Fig. 10.19 Colonoscopic appearance of cobblestoning. Courtesy of Dr. D. P. Jewell.

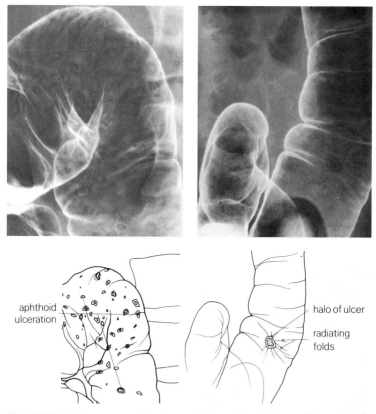

Fig. 10.20 Barium enemas showing multiple aphthoid ulcers with a distinctive dark halo around the superficial ulcer (left). The bowel and intervening mucosa have a normal configuration. A large single aphthoid ulcer (right).

Radiology

The radiological features of Crohn's disease are diverse, reflecting its variable nature and distribution. There is no pathognomonic radiological sign of Crohn's disease and the changes may be seen in other inflammatory conditions, such as ulcerative colitis, amoebiasis, intestinal tuberculosis and yersiniosis. A radiological diagnosis of Crohn's disease rests on a combination of radiological features and the distribution of these changes taken together with clinical, laboratory and histopathological findings. Features that are highly suggestive of the condition include aphthoid ulceration (Fig. 10.20), pseudodiverticula formation (Fig. 10.21), deep fissuring ulceration

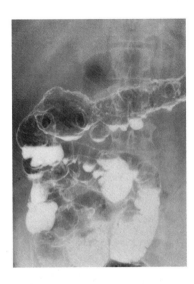

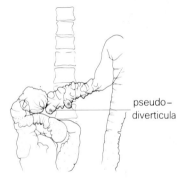

Fig. 10.21 Barium enema showing extensive pseudodiverticula formation in the transverse colon.

pseudo-
diverticula

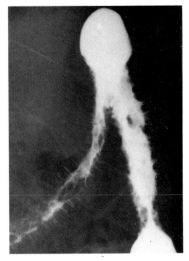

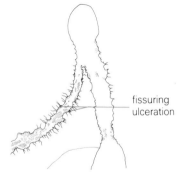

Fig. 10.22 Barium enema showing deep fissuring ulceration in the transverse colon.

fissuring
ulceration

47

(Fig. 10.22), skip lesions (Fig. 10.23), asymmetrical wall involvement (Fig. 10.24), relative rectal sparing on barium enema examination (Fig. 10.25) and the formation of strictures and, or, fistulae.

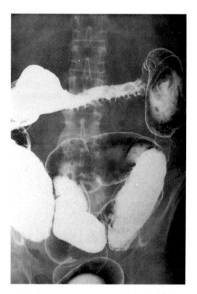

Fig. 10.23 Barium enema in advanced Crohn's disease showing a 'skip lesion' between two diseased segments in the descending colon.

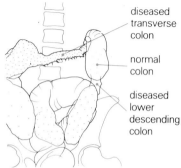

diseased transverse colon

normal colon

diseased lower descending colon

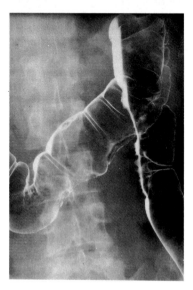

Fig. 10.24 Barium enema showing asymmetrical involvement of the bowel wall. There is linear ulceration on the antimesenteric border of the transverse colon and fissuring ulceration in the descending colon with adjacent normal mucosa.

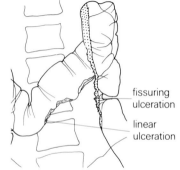

fissuring ulceration

linear ulceration

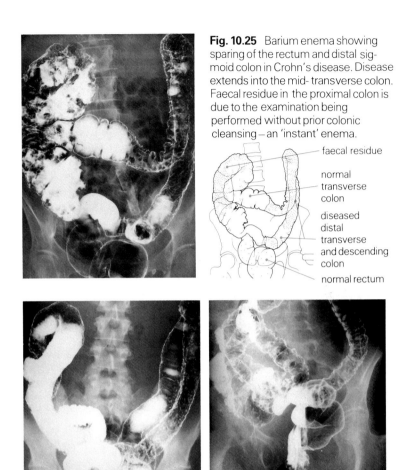

Fig. 10.25 Barium enema showing sparing of the rectum and distal sigmoid colon in Crohn's disease. Disease extends into the mid- transverse colon. Faecal residue in the proximal colon is due to the examination being performed without prior colonic cleansing – an 'instant' enema.

- faecal residue
- normal transverse colon
- diseased distal transverse and descending colon
- normal rectum

Fig. 10.26 Barium enemas showing extensive ulceration throughout the colon (left) and diffuse ulceration with an anal fistula and rectal sparing (right).

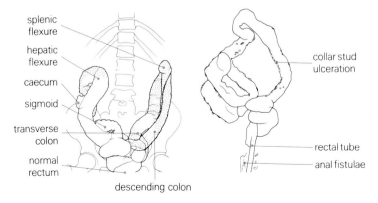

- splenic flexure
- hepatic flexure
- caecum
- sigmoid
- transverse colon
- normal rectum
- descending colon

- collar stud ulceration
- rectal tube
- anal fistulae

Ulceration may be extensive (Fig. 10.26), or discrete with a superficial ulcer surrounded by normal mucosa (Figs. 10.27 & 10.28). The combination of linear ulceration and transverse fissuring with submucosal oedema and inflammation produces the 'cobblestone' appearance (Fig. 10.29), but this is not a common appearance on double contrast enema.

Ileocaecal involvement often produces a thickened ileocaecal sphincter with fistulous tracts and deformity of the caecum (Fig. 10.30).

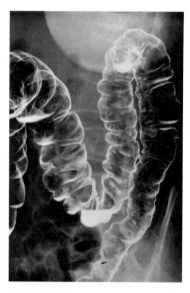

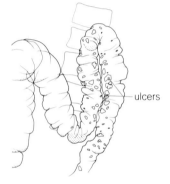

Fig. 10.27 Barium enema showing large serpiginous ulcers clearly demarcated from normal mucosa.

ulcers

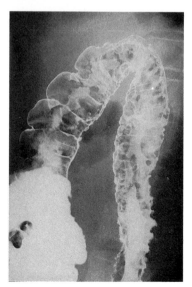

Fig. 10.28 Barium enema showing a sepiginous ulcer demarcated from normal mucosa.

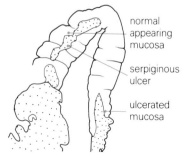

normal appearing mucosa

serpiginous ulcer

ulcerated mucosa

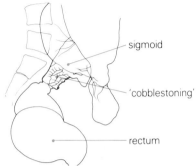

Fig. 10.29 Barium enema radiograph showing a short segment of 'cobblestoning' in the sigmoid colon, produced by longitudinal ulceration and transverse fissuring.

sigmoid

'cobblestoning'

rectum

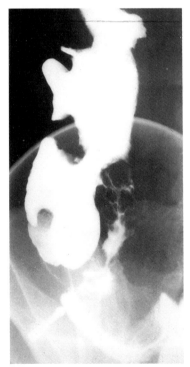

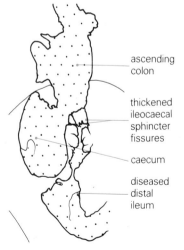

Fig. 10.30 Barium follow through demonstrating marked thickening of the ileocaecal sphincter and deep fissuring ulcers/fistulas through the sphincter.

ascending colon

thickened ileocaecal sphincter fissures

caecum

diseased distal ileum

Ileal ulceration is commonly associated with caecal disease, but other parts of the alimentary tract may be involved including the stomach, duodenum (Fig. 10.31) and oesophagus (Fig. 10.32).

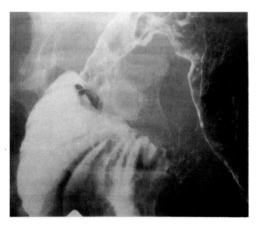

Fig. 10.31 Barium meal in Crohn's disease showing gastroduodenal involvement. There is some aphthoid ulceration in the antrum, a patulous pylorus with ulceration and narrowing of the second and third parts of the duodenum, and a dilated segment in the lower part of the descending limb of the loop.

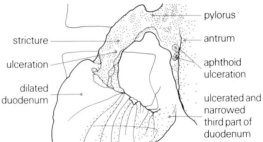

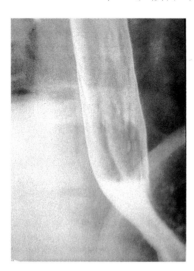

Fig. 10.32 Barium swallow showing oesophageal involvement in Crohn's disease. Courtesy of Dr. H. Kressel.

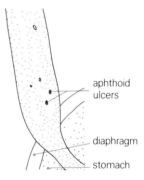

Fistulae require radiological confirmation and delineation, especially if surgery is planned. Various examples are shown in Figs. 10.33-10.35.

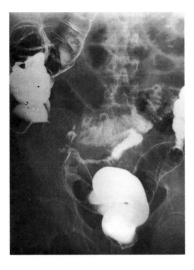

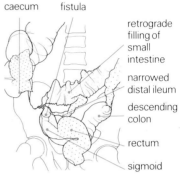

Fig. 10.33 Barium enema showing an enterocolic fistula between the ileum and sigmoid colon.

caecum   fistula

retrograde filling of small intestine

narrowed distal ileum

descending colon

rectum

sigmoid

Fig. 10.34 Barium enema showing a rectovaginal fistula.

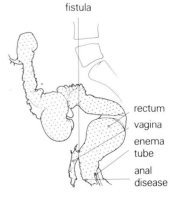

fistula

rectum
vagina
enema tube
anal disease

Pathology

Crohn's disease affects all layers of the bowel wall and tends to produce narrowing and thickening of any involved segment. The classical finding is a stricture of the distal 10-20cm of the ileum. However, the small and large intestine may be affected at any site. The strictures vary in length from a few, to up to 30cm and can be solitary or multiple (Fig. 10.36). In involved areas, whether strictured or not, the mucosa is ulcerated in a linear fashion. Surviving mucosa is often raised by submucosal oedema,

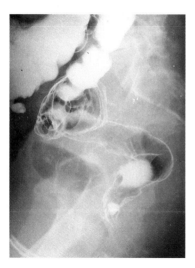

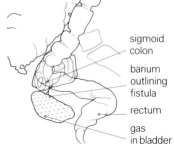

Fig. 10.35 Barium enema showing a vesicocolic fistula. A short fistulous tract extends from the diseased sigmoid to the air-filled bladder.

sigmoid colon

barium outlining fistula

rectum

gas in bladder

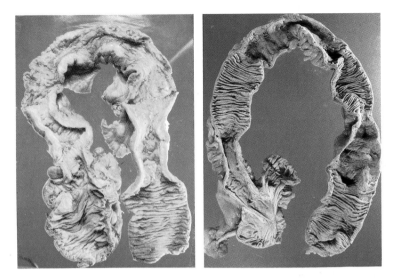

Fig. 10.36 Two specimens of intestine showing the typical features of Crohn's disease. The distal ileum (left) is thickened and narrowed. The colon (right) has strictures separated by normal mucosa.

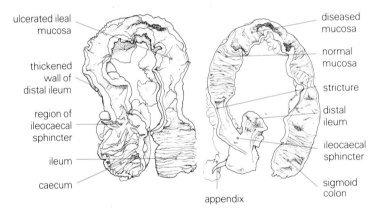

ulcerated ileal mucosa

thickened wall of distal ileum

region of ileocaecal sphincter

ileum

caecum

appendix

diseased mucosa

normal mucosa

stricture

distal ileum

ileocaecal sphincter

sigmoid colon

producing a cobblestone appearance (Fig. 10.37). Segments of normal bowel typically occur between affected regions (skip lesions). Loops of bowel, may be bound together by fibrosis, and fistulae can develop between such loops (Fig. 10.38). In the large bowel the disease most often involves the right side with rectal sparing, but in the elderly there may be distal left-sided involvement. Less commonly there is a total

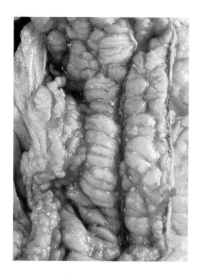

Fig. 10.37 Oedematous colonic mucosa in Crohn's colitis showing the 'cobblestone' appearance.

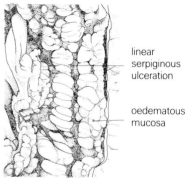

linear serpiginous ulceration

oedematous mucosa

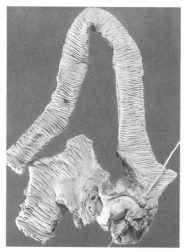

Fig. 10.38 Macroscopic appearance of an enterocolic fistula. A fistula has developed between the diseased distal ileum and the adherent sigmoid colon.

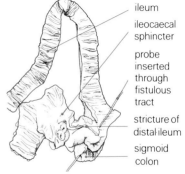

ileum

ileocaecal sphincter

probe inserted through fistulous tract

stricture of distal ileum

sigmoid colon

colitis. Complications such as toxic dilatation and carcinoma are much rarer in Crohn's disease than in ulcerative colitis. The earliest lesions of Crohn's disease are thought to be aphthoid ulcers, which are tiny mucosal lesions representing ulceration overlying lymphoid follicles (Fig. 10.39).

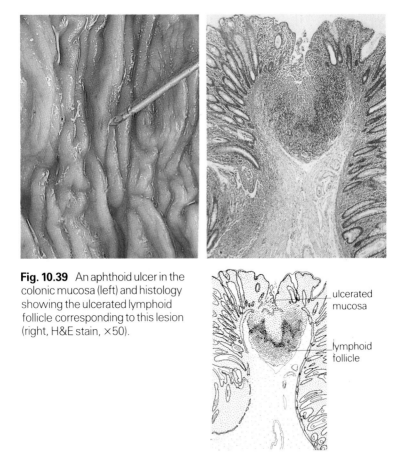

Fig. 10.39 An aphthoid ulcer in the colonic mucosa (left) and histology showing the ulcerated lymphoid follicle corresponding to this lesion (right, H&E stain, ×50).

ulcerated mucosa

lymphoid follicle

Histopathological examination in Crohn's disease shows discrete granulomas, fissuring ulceration, submucosal fibrosis and transmural inflammation (Figs. 10.40-10.42). In addition to obvious mucosal inflammation, aggregates of lymphocytes are scattered through the bowel wall, and often occur as 'beads' of inflammation along the serosa. The granulomas are discrete and do not caseate. They are present in up to 60% of cases, and may be seen at any site in the gut wall. The fissuring ulceration usually extends into the submucosa and less often through the full thickness of the muscle. Fissuring ulcers may lead to the formation of fistulae. The strictures of Crohn's disease are

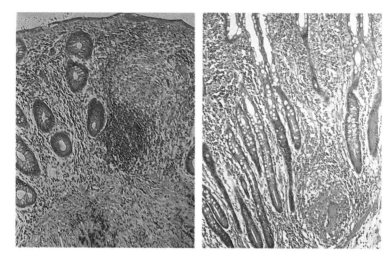

Fig. 10.40 Sections of colonic mucosa (left) and ileal mucosa (right) showing characteristic granulomas. H&E stain, ×120.

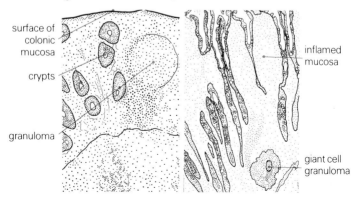

surface of colonic mucosa

crypts

granuloma

inflamed mucosa

giant cell granuloma

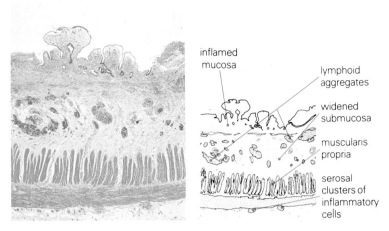

inflamed mucosa

lymphoid aggregates

widened submucosa

muscularis propria

serosal clusters of inflammatory cells

Fig. 10.41 Colonic mucosa showing marked inflammation. Aggregates of lymphocytes and other inflammatory cells are seen in the submucosa and serosa, indicating transmural involvement. H&E stain, ×25.

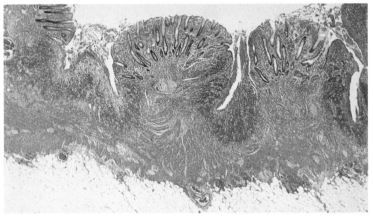

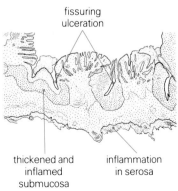

fissuring ulceration

thickened and inflamed submucosa

inflammation in serosa

Fig. 10.42 Colonic histology showing the typical fissuring ulceration of Crohn's disease with transmural inflammation. H&E stain, ×12.

produced by submucosal fibrosis and reduplication, as well as disorganisation of the muscularis mucosae (Fig. 10.43).

The patchy involvement of the gut produces sampling errors in assessments of biopsies. The sigmoidoscopic appearances may be normal with the disease apparently limited to the small intestine, but a rectal biopsy may still yield a diagnostic granuloma.

The histology of extra-intestinal sites of Crohn's disease also shows non-specific inflammation in which granulomas may be found.

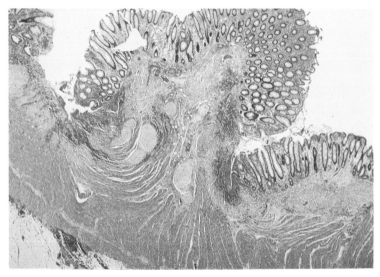

enlarged
submucosal
nerves   ulceration   mucosa

inflammatory
aggregate
in serosa

submucosal
inflammation
and fibrosis

Fig. 10.43 Colonic histology in Crohn's disease showing ulceration, submucosal fibrosis and neural hyperplasia. H&E stain, ×12.

11.
Colon IV
Ulcerative Colitis

Ulcerative colitis (UC) is a disorder of unknown aetiology characterised by inflammation of the colonic mucosa. In the West UC affects 40-80 people per 100,000 and together with Crohn's disease is classified as non-specific inflammatory bowel disease. The inflammatory process invariably affects the rectum and extends in continuity to involve a

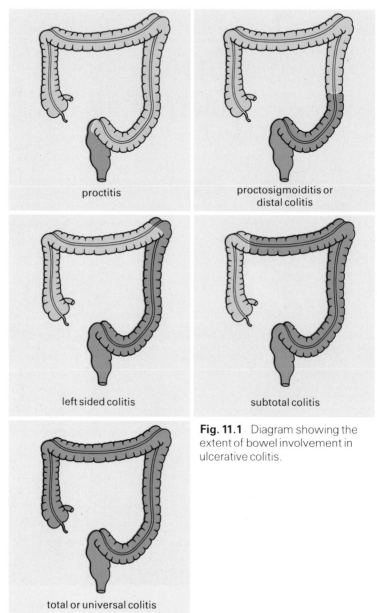

proctitis

proctosigmoiditis or distal colitis

left sided colitis

subtotal colitis

total or universal colitis

Fig. 11.1 Diagram showing the extent of bowel involvement in ulcerative colitis.

greater or lesser extent of the proximal colon such that a patient may have proctitis, proctosigmoiditis, left-sided disease, or sub-total or total colitis (Fig. 11.1).

Ulcerative colitis shares many similarities with colonic Crohn's disease but there are also several differences (Figs. 11.2 & 11.3).

Ulcerative colitis and colonic Crohn's disease – similarities

1. Age group affected.
2. Worldwide geographical and racial distribution.
3. Occurrence of both diseases in different individuals from same family.
4. Clinical features may be identical (particularly in colonic Crohn's disease).
5. Treatment.

Fig. 11.2 Table showing the major similarities between ulcerative colitis and Crohn's disease.

Ulcerative colitis and colonic Crohn's disease – differences

1. Incidence of UC is static; Crohn's is increasing.
2. Only colon affected in UC; Crohn's can also affect the small bowel.
3. UC has a marked tendency to relapse and remit; Crohn's is similar but less marked.
4. Clinical features of abdominal mass, signs of malabsorption, fistula formation and gross perianal disease do not occur in UC.
5. Radiological features – UC changes affect rectum and proximal colon in continuity; deep fissuring and aphthoid ulceration, 'skip' lesions and small bowel involvement are features of Crohn's disease.
6. Histological features – transmural inflammation, fissuring, granulomas and goblet cell preservation are features of Crohn's disease. UC is characterised by mucosal inflammation, crypt abscesses and goblet cell depletion.

Fig. 11.3 Table showing the major differences between ulcerative colitis and Crohn's disease.

However, in some patients it may be impossible to decide if the disease is UC or Crohn's colitis.

The cause of UC is unknown and although stress and allergy, particularly to food products, have received much attention in the past, there is little evidence to suggest they play a primary role in initiating the disease. At present, as with Crohn's disease, the evidence favours a role for an unusual infective agent, such as a small RNA virus, although the case is far from proven. Some patients have a family history of either ulcerative colitis, Crohn's disease or ankylosing spondylitis (Fig. 11.4) although there is no simple pattern of inheritance and the likelihood of a patient's child inheriting inflammatory bowel disease is less than 5%.

The clinical presentation of ulcerative colitis depends on the length of colon involved and severity of the episode. The attack may be classified as mild, moderate or severe according to the symptoms and the presence or absence of systemic features, such as pyrexia (Fig. 11.5). UC is characterised by relapses and remissions, although in a small number of cases the symptoms are continuous. Most patients present with diarrhoea associated with the passage of blood and mucus. Tenesmus is common and in severe cases extra-intestinal manifestations such as arthropathy, iritis, erythema nodosum or pyoderma gangrenosum occur (Fig. 11.6).

Physical examination is often unrewarding, although in severe cases the patient is pyrexial, anaemic and may be tender over the distribution of the colon on palpation. Perianal disease is uncommon and when it does occur it is usually mild and consists of shallow fissuring or maceration due to the frequency of defaecation and soiling.

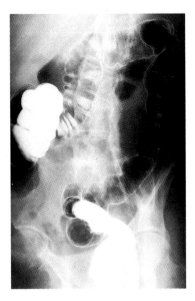

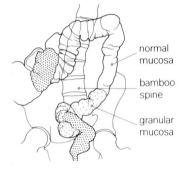

Fig. 11.4 A barium enema in mild distal ulcerative colitis showing the typical 'bamboo' spine of ankylosing spondylitis.

normal mucosa

bamboo spine

granular mucosa

	Mild	Moderate	Severe
Bowel frequency	<4 daily	4-6	>6 daily
Blood in stool	±	+	++
Temperature	Normal	Intermediate between mild and severe	>37.8°C on 2 days out of 4
Pulse rate	Normal	Intermediate between mild and severe	>90 beats per minute
Haemoglobin	Normal	Intermediate between mild and severe	<75%
ESR	<30mm in first hour	Intermediate between mild and severe	>30mm in first hour

Fig. 11.5 Classification of the features of mild, moderate and severe ulcerative colitis.

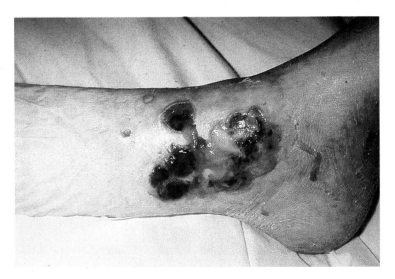

Fig. 11.6 Pyoderma gangrenosum. Courtesy of Mr. J. Alexander-Williams

The most useful investigation is sigmoidoscopy since mucosal inflammation is almost invariably visible. This can be mild, with only hyperaemia and granularity of the mucosa (Fig. 11.7) or more severe with contact bleeding (Fig. 11.8) or even extensive ulceration

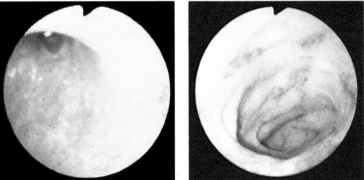

Fig. 11.7 Sigmoidscopy showing hyperaemia and mucosal granularity in ulcerative colitis. Courtesy of Dr. C. Williams.

Fig. 11.8 Sigmoidoscopy showing contact bleeding in ulcerative colitis. Courtesy of Dr. C. Williams.

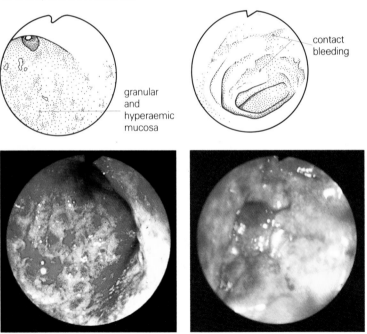

Fig. 11.9 Sigmoidoscopy in ulcerative colitis showing extensive ulceration (left, courtesy of Prof. R. Hunt) and oedematous and ulcerated congested folds with contact bleeding (right).

(Fig. 11.9). A rectal mucosal biopsy is taken at the same time as sigmoidoscopy for histological confirmation of the diagnosis and differentiation from colonic Crohn's disease (see below). Further initial investigations must include stool culture to exclude infective agents which may resemble the clinical and sigmoidoscopic features of the disease. These include *Salmonella spp.*, *Shigella spp.*, *Entamoeba histolytica* and *Campylobacter spp.* A blood count, sedimentation rate and liver function tests should also be performed at the outset.

A plain abdominal radiograph is very useful in acute UC. The presence of faecal shadows in a colonic segment suggests the absence

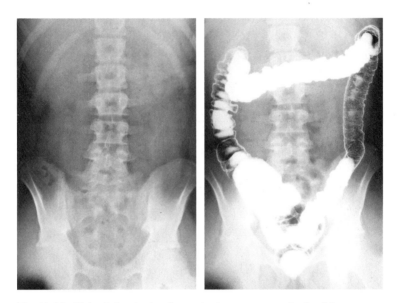

Fig. 11.10 Plain abdominal radiograph of an acute attack of colitis showing only a small pocket of gas in the caecum and no formed residue (left). The abdomen has an empty appearance. An 'instant' enema (ie. without any prior bowel preparation) performed at the same time shows extensive active colitis with a granular mucosa (right).

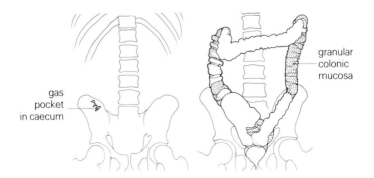

gas pocket in caecum

granular colonic mucosa

of mucosal inflammation of that area. The colon may be completely empty of gas and faecal residue suggesting active disease of the whole colon (Fig. 11.10). The amount of gas in the bowel tends to increase with the severity of the colitis. Intraluminal gas will define a configuration of the mucosal surface and the width of the bowel (Fig. 11.11). With severe ulceration the mucosal surface becomes coarsely irregular and haustration is absent. Dilatation of more than 5 cm diameter suggests that the ulcers are penetrating deeply into the colonic muscle, which places the patient at grave risk of colonic perforation or toxic megacolon. Patients with active distal disease and a relatively normal proximal colon may develop proximal faecal retention and pass frequent loose stools with blood and mucus (Fig. 11.12).

An air-contrast barium enema will demonstrate the extent and severity of the colitis (Fig. 11.13) and provides a useful record of the fluctuations of the disease. In relatively acute disease the patient should

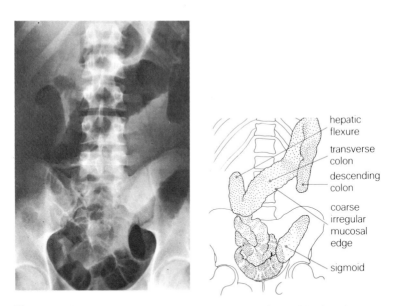

Fig. 11.11 Plain abdominal radiograph in severe active colitis showing extensive gas in the large and small bowel and no formed faecal residue. The transverse colon is dilated and has a coarse mucosal edge, without haustra. These changes indicate deep ulceration into the colonic muscle layer. Following colectomy, early changes of toxic megacolon were found histologically.

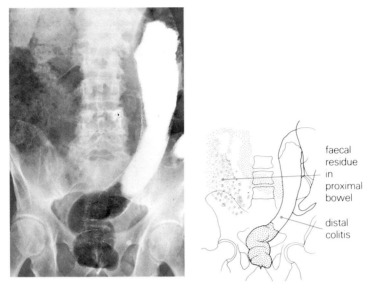

Fig. 11.12 'Instant' enema showing proximal faecal retention with active distal colitis.

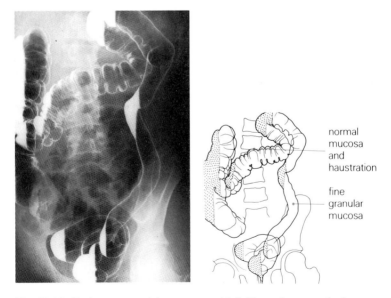

Fig. 11.13 Barium enema (air-contrast with full bowel preparation) showing fine granularity of the mucosa, extending in continuity to the splenic flexure. This is a lateral decubitus view, hence the barium fluid levels.

have a so-called 'instant' enema (Fig. 11.14) which is a double-contrast study performed without any prior preparation. Rectal balloon catheters should not be used and, due to the small risk of perforation, it is probably best to delay examination for three days following rectal biopsy.

Barium enema examination is contra-indicated in fulminating colitis. In chronic low grade ulcerative colitis, when there is a risk of malignancy, a double contrast barium enema with full bowel preparation should be performed.

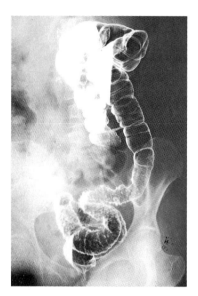

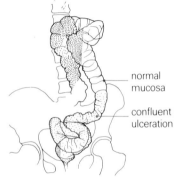

Fig. 11.14 'Instant' enema in an acute attack of ulcerative colitis with distal ulceration. The ulcers are shallow and confluent, and there is an abrupt transition to normal mucosa in the lower descending colon.

normal mucosa

confluent ulceration

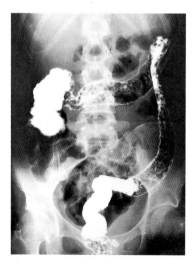

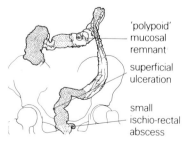

Fig. 11.15 'Instant' enema showing pseudopolyposis. Extensive ulceration has left scattered mucosal remnants creating a polypoid mucosal surface.

'polypoid' mucosal remnant

superficial ulceration

small ischio-rectal abscess

The radiographic features of ulcerative colitis combine mucosal changes with abnormal configuration of the bowel wall. The typical abnormality is granularity of the mucosa (see Fig. 11.13). Ulceration is seen only in acute attacks (see Fig. 11.14). Where this is extensive, the remaining inflamed oedematous mucosa may assume a pseudopolypoid appearance (Fig. 11.15). Healing after an episode of ulceration may leave the patient with post-inflammatory polyps (Fig. 11.16). In total colitis there may be inflammation of the terminal ileum, known as 'backwash ileitis' (Fig. 11.17). This form of ileitis does not have the

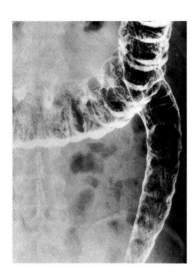

Fig. 11. 16 Barium enema showing post-inflammatory polyposis involving the left herniation in inactive ulcerative colitis.

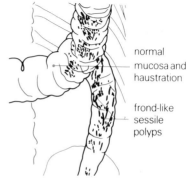

normal mucosa and haustration

frond-like sessile polyps

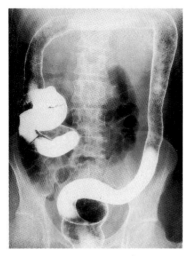

Fig. 11. 17 'Instant' double-contrast barium enema in total ulcerative colitis. The distal ileum is dilated with a granular surface indicating reflux ('backwash') ileitis.

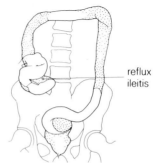

reflux ileitis

same implications as that in Crohn's disease, and it either resolves with treatment directly, or spontaneously following colectomy.

Complications

There are a number of short and long-term complications of ulcerative colitis. The initial complications include the extra-intestinal manifestations of the disease outlined above, or the development of a sacroiliitis (Fig. 11.18) or ankylosing spondylitis (see Fig. 11.4). Acute severe disease may be complicated by haemorrhage, the development of a toxic megacolon and perforation.

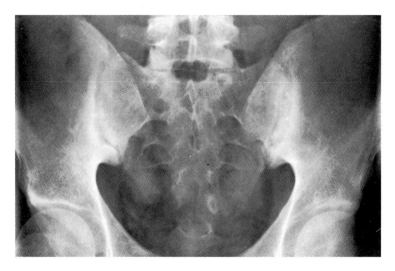

Fig. 11.18 Pelvic radiograph in ulcerative colitis showing bilateral sacroiliitis with marked sclerosis and irregularity of the joints. The spine is normal with no evidence of ankylosing spondylitis.

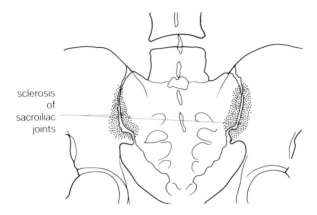

sclerosis of sacroiliac joints

Toxic megacolon results in a deterioration in the patients' condition with the development of tachycardia, abdominal tenderness and distension. A plain abdominal radiograph demonstrates the dilated colon with mucosal islands (Fig. 11.19). In this situation the patient frequently requires a colectomy (Fig. 11.20) since perforation of the colon may be imminent. Nevertheless, some patients with toxic megacolon resolve with conservative management and the decision to operate is a matter of clinical judgement.

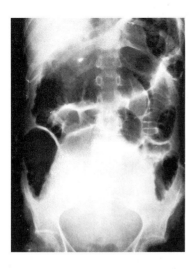

Fig. 11.19 Plain abdominal radiograph in toxic megacolon showing a grossly dilated transverse colon with mucosal islands in the ascending colon. Concommitant distension of the small bowel is associated with very active colitis.

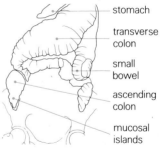

- stomach
- transverse colon
- small bowel
- ascending colon
- mucosal islands

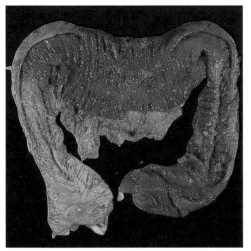

Fig. 11.20 Colectomy specimen in toxic megacolon. Courtesy of Mr. J. Alexander-Williams.

Failure of an acute severe relapse to settle with optimum medical treatment is also an indication for surgical removal of a diseased colon. The surgical procedure is either a panproctocolectomy with fashioning of a Brooke ileostomy (Fig. 11.21), or colectomy with preservation of the rectal stump and a subsequent ileo-rectal anastomosis. There are several advantages and disadvantages in both procedures and the decision as to which operation to perform varies with individual

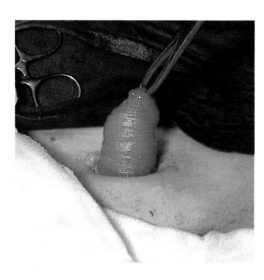

Fig. 11.21 Brooke ileostomy. Courtesy of Mr. J. Alexander-Williams.

Hepatobiliary complications of inflammatory bowel disease	
Biliary	Pericholangitis Primary sclerosing cholangitis (rare in Crohn's) Bile duct carcinoma Gall stones (Crohn's only)
Hepato-cellular	Chronic active hepatitis Cirrhosis
Miscellaneous	Fatty change Amyloid Granulomata

Fig. 11.22 Table listing the hepato-biliary complications on inflammatory bowel disease.

patients. More recent innovations include sphincter preserving operations with formation of an 'ileal' rectal pouch. Following colectomy for acute colitis, previously severely ill patients rapidly regain weight and full health.

The longer term complications of ulcerative colitis include a variety of hepato-biliary disorders (Fig. 11.22) of which the most common is sclerosing cholangitis (Fig. 11.23). This chronic fibrosing inflammatory process affects the intra- and extra-hepatic biliary systems, which leads to chronic cholestasis and, in severe cases, portal hypertension and its sequelae.

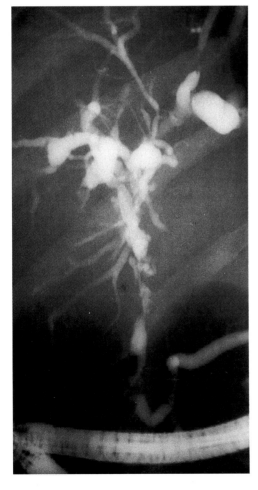

Fig. 11.23 ERCP in sclerosing cholangitis showing intrahepatic and common bile ducts with multiple strictures.

irregular and
strictured
intrahepatic
and common
bile ducts

endoscope   pancreatic
duct

The most important long-term complication of the disease is the development of a carcinoma of the colon. The risk is greatest in patients who have had a total colitis for 10 years or more, the risk increasing with the length of time the disease has been present (Fig. 11.24). For patients with sub-total, or left-sided disease the risk appears to be delayed by approximately 10 years. It was originally thought that juvenile onset of colitis also increased the risk, however this may only be an apparent increase due to the longer follow-up inherent in patients with early onset of the disease.

The carcinoma may be multifocal, or single. It usually presents as an infiltrative plaque, less commonly as a polypoid mass, or a stricture (Fig. 11.25). Colonic strictures in patients with ulcerative colitis are not necessarily malignant and colonoscopy is necessary to determine whether a stricture demonstrated on barium enema is benign (Fig. 11. 26) or malignant (Fig. 11.27).

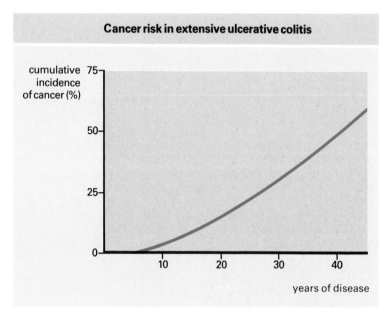

Fig. 11.24 Graph showing the increasing risk of cancer in ulcerative colitis.

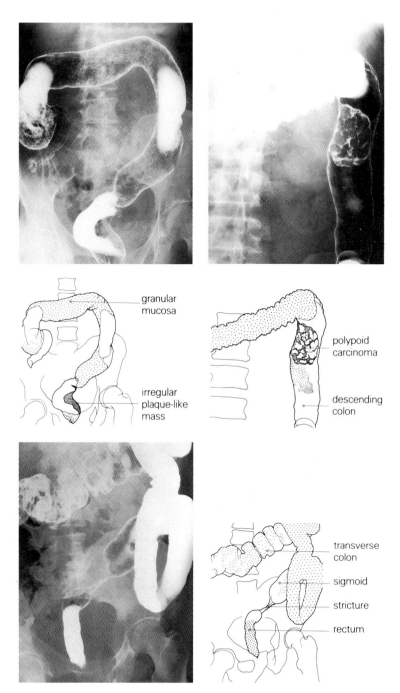

Fig. 11.25 Barium enema radiographs showing carcinoma in ulcerative colitis presenting as an infiltrative plaque (left), a polypoid mass (right) and a stricture (bottom).

While colonoscopy is unnecessary in the routine management of ulcerative colitis, it is important in the long-term follow up of the disease. It has been shown that prior to the development of a carcinoma in susceptible individuals, dysplastic changes occur and these can be detected histologically on rectal, or colonic biopsy. The dysplastic changes may be patchy and prone to sampling error. Individuals at risk should therefore have periodic colonoscopy and biopsy of the entire colon, starting 8 to 10 years after the onset of the disease in patients who have total colitis, and from 15 to 20 years in patients with left-sided or sub-total disease.

Because the carcinomas which develop in ulcerative colitis tend to be shallow plaque-like tumours, the radiological features of annular or large polypoid cancer are not seen so commonly. Any small irregular polypoid lesion on barium enema must be viewed with considerable

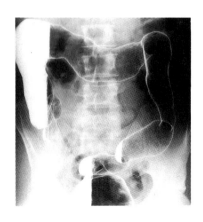

Fig. 11.26 Barium enema (lateral decubitus view) showing the granular mucosa and complete absence of haustra, which confirms total colitis. Two short strictures, are present in the descending colon. There are no malignant features on radiology, and the strictures were confirmed by colonoscopy to be benign.

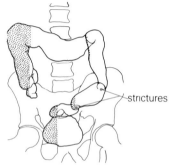

strictures

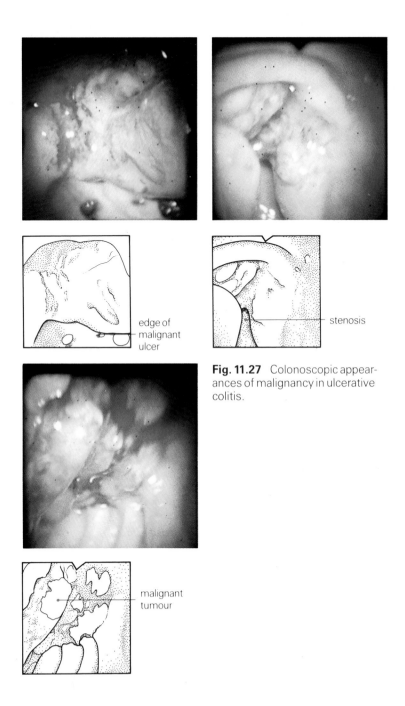

edge of
malignant
ulcer

stenosis

Fig. 11.27 Colonoscopic appearances of malignancy in ulcerative colitis.

malignant
tumour

79

suspicion (Fig. 11.28), particularly if there is indrawing of the base. Only gross dysplasia will be visible radiologically and for this reason a routine barium enema is not advised for the investigation of possible dysplasia. Double-contrast barium enema can be performed alternatively with colonoscopy in the long-term follow up of patients. However, the subtle mucosal abnormalities that can accompany some dysplastic changes can also be missed at colonoscopy.

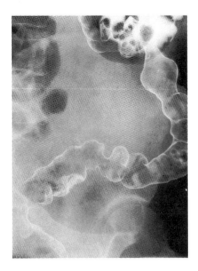

Fig. 11.28 Barium enema showing a suspicious irregular polypoid lesion, which proved to be an early carcinoma.

Fig. 11.29 Macroscopic appearance of the colon in UC showing the typical even pattern of involvement with sparing of the right side.

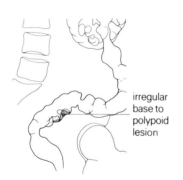

irregular base to polypoid lesion

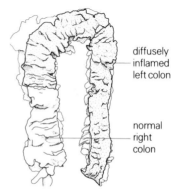

diffusely inflamed left colon

normal right colon

Pathology

Macroscopically the colon in ulcerative colitis is usually normal from the serosal aspect, apart from obvious shortening. Typically, the mucosa has an even pattern of abnormality invariably involving the rectum (Figs. 11.29 & 11.30) and extending proximally over a varying length of colon. The precise mucosal appearance depends on the activity of the disease. Most commonly the rectal mucosa has a red, granular, friable

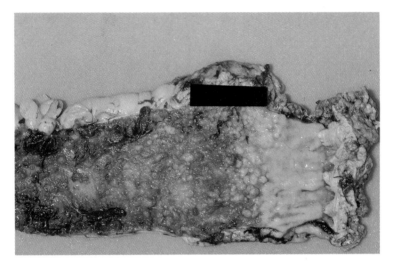

Fig. 11.30 Macroscopic appearance of the rectum in severe ulcerative colitis showing inflamed mucosa surviving as islands between the intercommunicating areas of ulceration. The mucosa immediately proximal to the anal margin, although intact, is also histologically inflamed.

appearance. Ulceration may be minimal, patchy or extensive with only islands of surviving mucosa remaining (Figs. 11.31-11.34). Between ulcers the mucosa is always abnormal. In total colonic involvement 'backwash ileitis' may be recognised (see above) and the distal 5-25 cm of ileum may then appear inflamed.

Fig. 11.31 Macroscopic appearance in early active ulcerative colitis showing a typical, even, red granular mucosa. Early on the mucosa is not necessarily ulcerated.

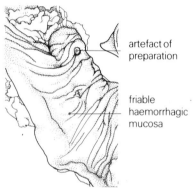

artefact of preparation

friable haemorrhagic mucosa

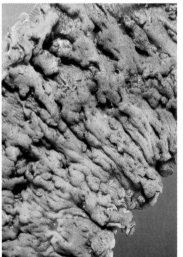

Fig. 11.32 Macroscopic appearance in total colitis showing extensive ulceration.

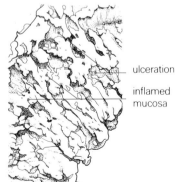

ulceration

inflamed mucosa

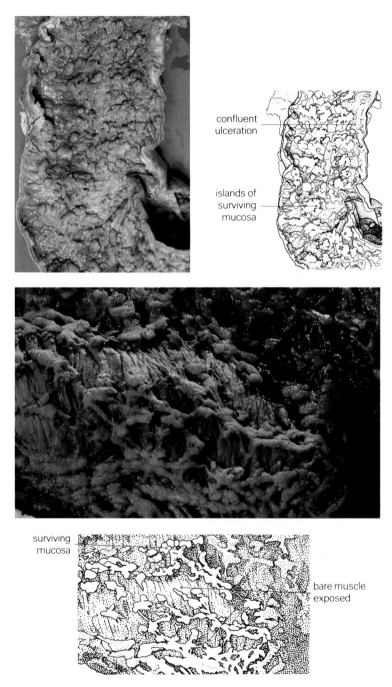

Fig. 11.33 Macroscopic appearances showing confluent ulceration and large areas of exposed muscle wall.

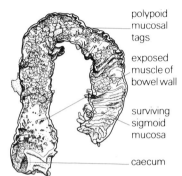

Fig. 11.34 Macroscopic appearance in severe total ulcerative colitis. The rectum and sigmoid colon may appear to be relatively spared (as in this example), if steroid enemas have been used.

polypoid mucosal tags

exposed muscle of bowel wall

surviving sigmoid mucosa

caecum

Fig. 11.35 Macroscopic appearances showing the featureless mucosa of long-standing but now quiescent ulcerative colitis.

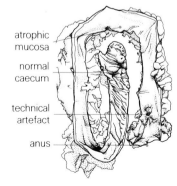

atrophic mucosa

normal caecum

technical artefact

anus

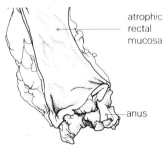

atrophic rectal mucosa

anus

In a quiescent phase of longstanding disease the mucosa appears flat, pale and featureless (Fig. 11.35). Because not all regions of the bowel may be equally active a misleading segmental pattern of the disease may be suggested (Fig. 11.36).

The presence of numerous 'pseudopolyps' (Fig. 11.37) which are often little more than mucosal tags, indicate healed episodes of previous severe ulceration. Fibrous strictures are not a feature of ulcerative colitis and a stricture may indicate malignancy, or simply muscular thickening.

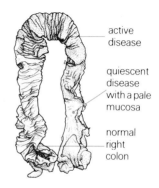

Fig. 11.36 Macroscopic appearance of the colon showing variable involvement of different segments which gives the false impression of segmental disease.

active disease

quiescent disease with a pale mucosa

normal right colon

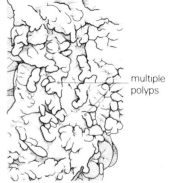

Fig. 11.37 Inflammatory pseudopolyps which mark previous severe ulceration.

multiple polyps

Histology shows that, in contrast to Crohn's disease, all the inflammatory changes are confined to the mucosa (Fig. 11.38). The ulceration can extend into the submucosa, but there is no fissuring. In

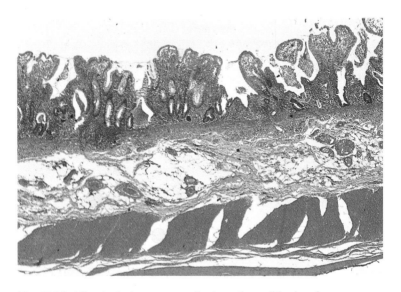

Fig. 11.38 Histological appearance in ulcerative colitis showing inflammation limited to the mucosa. H & E stain, × 12.

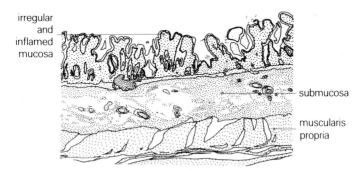

active disease intact mucosa is inflamed with prominent crypt abscesses (Figs. 11.39 & 11.40), mucin depletion and derangement of the crypt pattern. This rarely returns to normal and mucosal atrophy is

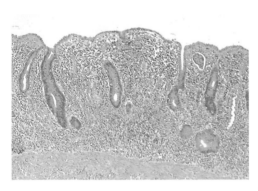

Fig. 11.39 Histological appearance in active ulcerative colitis. The crypts are short, irregular and pushed apart by the diffuse inflammation which ceases at the muscularis. The goblet cells are depleted. H & E stain, × 50.

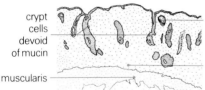

crypt cells devoid of mucin

muscularis

crypt abscess

diffuse inflammation throughout lamina propria

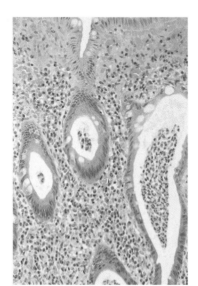

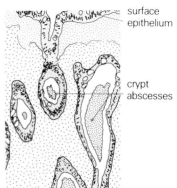

Fig. 11.40 Colonic histology in ulcerative colitis showing crypt abscesses. These are common in UC but are also seen in other forms of inflammatory bowel disease. H & E stain, × 120.

surface epithelium

crypt abscesses

typical of longstanding quiescent ulcerative colitis (Figs. 11.41 & 11.42). A series of endoscopic biopsies will be abnormal showing inflammation, perhaps of varying severity. The continuous pattern of

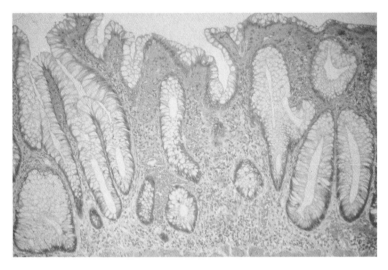

Fig. 11.41 Histological appearance of ulcerative colitis going into remission. The crypt architecture is irregular but the mucin in the goblet cells is restored to normal. H & E stain, × 75.

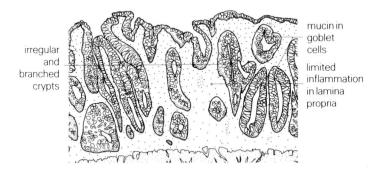

irregular and branched crypts

mucin in goblet cells

limited inflammation in lamina propria

disease contrasts with the uneven pattern of involvement seen in Crohn's disease, when normal mucosal biopsies may be interspaced between abnormal areas (Fig. 11.43).

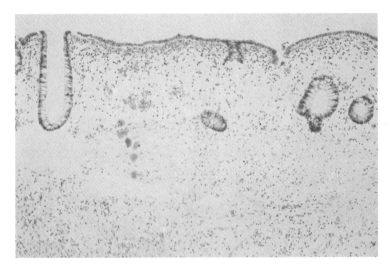

Fig. 11.42 Atrophic rectal mucosa in chronic ulcerative colitis: the crypts have failed to regenerate and the lamina propria is empty, with few inflammatory cells. H & E stain, × 75.

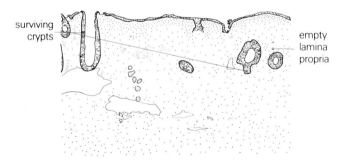

surviving crypts

empty lamina propria

Carcinoma as a complication in colitis has already been noted. The interest lies firstly in the unusual flat nature of many such lesions, as opposed to the polypoid adenomatous origin of carcinoma on the non-colitic bowel (Figs. 11.44 & 11.45). This poses problems for the

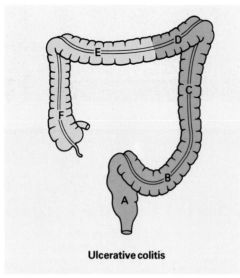

Ulcerative colitis

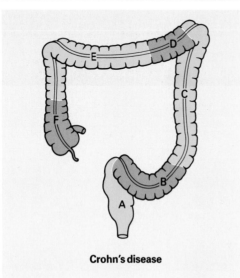

Crohn's disease

Fig. 11.43 Diagram contrasting the difference in distribution of inflammation in typical Crohn's disease and ulcerative colitis. In UC biopsies from sites A to D will all be abnormal and E, F, normal. In Crohn's disease the distribution is irregular. A, C and E are normal but B, D and F are abnormal.

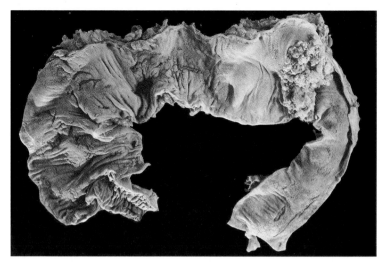

Fig. 11.44 A subtotal colectomy in longstanding ulcerative colitis showing a carcinoma and raised roughened areas, which are commonly sites of dysplasia.

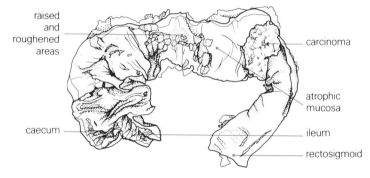

raised and roughened areas

carcinoma

atrophic mucosa

caecum

ileum

rectosigmoid

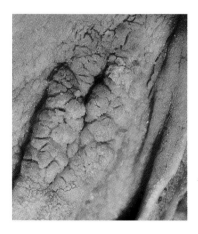

Fig. 11.45 Macroscopic appearance of plaque-like areas of high grade dysplasia which are easily overlooked when flat and ill-defined as in this example.

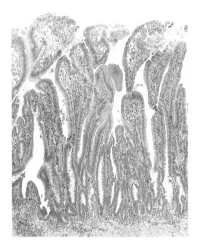

Fig. 11.46 Appearance of the dysplastic mucosa in ulcerative colitis. It is frequently thickened partly due to the process. It can produce quite a marked villiform configuration as in this example. H & E stain, × 50.

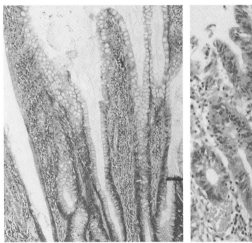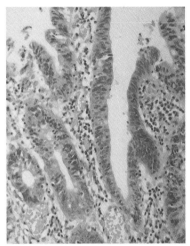

Fig. 11.47 Histological appearance of low grade dysplasia in the lower crypts (left) and high grade (severe) dysplasia in the colonic mucosa (right). In the high grade, the markedly abnormal nuclei show pleomorphism and pseudostratification. H & E stain, × 120.

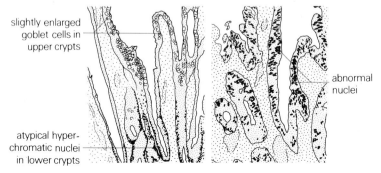

slightly enlarged goblet cells in upper crypts

atypical hyperchromatic nuclei in lower crypts

abnormal nuclei

radiologist and colonoscopist. Secondly, it is possible to screen for carcinoma by identifying foci of dysplasia in a biopsy (Figs. 11.46 – 11.49).

Severe dysplasia is easily recognised and should prompt a careful search for carcinoma throughout the colon. If this is negative but severe dysplasia is found on a repeat biopsy then consideration must be given to a prophylactic colectomy. Milder degrees of dysplasia are of less significance, though follow-up procedures should be adopted.

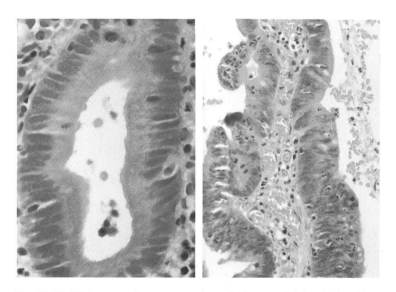

Fig. 11.48 High power views comparing mild (low grade) dysplasia with severe (high grade) dysplasia. In mild dysplasia the cells are hyperchromatic with mucin loss but nuclear polarity is regular. Polarity is completely lost in severe dysplasia. H & E stain, × 480.

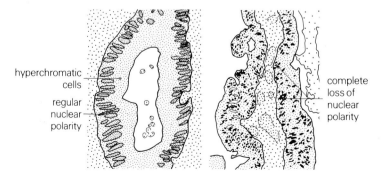

hyperchromatic cells

regular nuclear polarity

complete loss of nuclear polarity

Toxic megacolon is a life threatening complication of ulcerative colitis. The whole thickness of the colonic wall becomes involved and disintegration of the muscle coat occurs (Fig. 11.50). In this state the appearance is common to the many forms of colitis in which this complication can occur, for example, Crohn's disease, amoebic colitis, and pseudomembranous colitis. This is essentially 'end-stage' bowel in which the more subtle diagnostic features are masked by the severity of the inflammatory and degenerative processes.

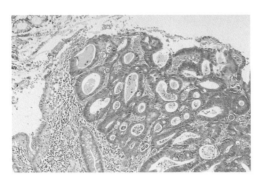

Fig. 11.49 Colonic biopsy in ulcerative colitis showing frank intramucosal carcinoma. It evolves through the grades of dysplasia in non-polypoid mucosa. This is emphasised by the uninvolved mucosa at the left margin. H & E stain, × 120.

uninvolved mucosa

carcinoma

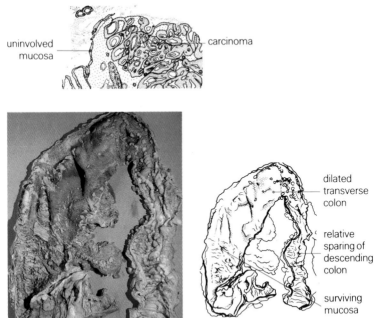

dilated transverse colon

relative sparing of descending colon

surviving mucosa

Fig. 11.50 Macroscopic appearance in toxic megacolon predominantly involving the ascending and transverse colon. The transverse colon and hepatic flexure are dilated and the mucosa has been lost.

12.
Colorectal Cancer, Polyps and Vascular Malformations

Colorectal Cancer

Colorectal cancer has an incidence of 38 per 100,000 in England and Wales and is one of the most common neoplasms in the Western world. It accounts for approximately 16,000 deaths per year in the United Kingdom, a figure exceeded only by death from carcinoma of the bronchus.

Although carcinoma of the colon and rectum can occasionally occur in young people, most patients are in the sixth and seventh decade. The sex incidence of colonic cancer is approximately equal, although, for rectal cancer, men are affected more commonly than women in a ratio of 2:1.

The cause of colorectal cancer is unknown, however, certain conditions predispose to its development and much recent interest has focused on the malignant transformation of adenomatous colonic polyps (*see below*). Other conditions which are associated with a higher risk of carcinoma include inherited disorders, such as familial polyposis coli and Gardner's syndrome, both of which are inherited as autosomal dominants. In addition to these specific entities there is a more general familial tendency for colorectal cancer with up to a four-fold increase of colonic cancer among relatives. Longstanding total, or extensive ulcerative colitis, also carries an increased risk of colonic cancer which may be as high as 30% after thirty years of the disease.

Environmental factors are believed to play a major part in the aetiology of colorectal cancer; it is virtually unknown in most of the third-world populations. It is postulated that as people in these areas have bulkier stools and more frequent bowel movements than people in the West, there is less time for carcinogens in the colonic lumen to be in contact with the mucosa. The nature of these carcinogens is at present unknown, although altered bacterial flora, its metabolites and secondary bile acids have been implicated. These factors may in turn be related to the amount of dietary fat and fibre, because the disease is more common in populations which consume a diet containing a large amount of animal fat but little cereal fibre.

A recessive genetic factor has been implicated in the aetiology of colorectal cancer. This factor supposedly controls the appearance of adenomatous polyps whilst environmental factors determine their subsequent growth and malignant transformation.

Between 60% and 80% of adenocarcinomas occur in the sigmoid colon or rectum (Fig. 12.1), with the remainder being almost evenly distributed through the rest of the colon (Fig. 12.2). The tumours spread by local invasion and by distant dissemination into blood vessels and lymphatics, or directly into the peritoneal cavity. A system of pathological staging described by Dukes in 1932 is a simple and useful prognostic indicator of survival following surgery (Fig. 12.3). At presentation approximately 15% of tumours are stage A, 40% stage B and 45% stage C. More complex classifications exist which take account of metastases to distant organs and vascular invasion; these additional factors make prognosis more difficult. About 5% of patients have more than one colonic cancer, and the incidence of synchronous cancers increases with the number of adenomas present.

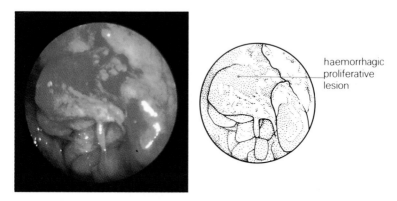

Fig. 12.1 Sigmoidoscopic view of a rectal carcinoma. A hemorrhagic proliferative lesion is protruding into the rectal lumen. Courtesy of Mr. P.J. Jeffery.

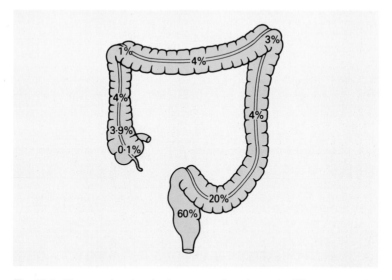

Fig. 12.2 Diagram showing the frequency of carcinoma in different parts of the colon.

Patients with colorectal cancer present with symptoms which largely depend on the site of the lesion. The typical presentation is a change in bowel habit with rectal bleeding, although abdominal pain and weight loss are also common. The symptoms may occur in any combination. Less often, symptoms of iron-deficiency anaemia are the sole mani-

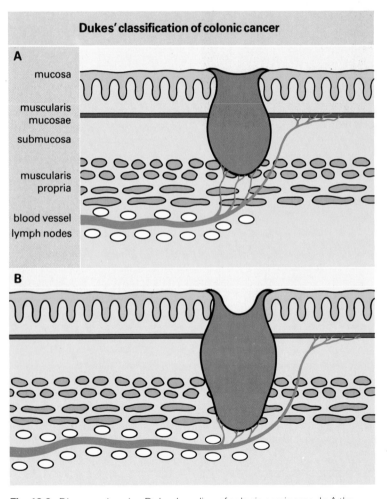

Fig. 12.3 Diagram showing Dukes' grading of colonic carcinoma. In A the tumour is confined to the bowel wall. In B it extends through the muscle coat but no lymph nodes are involved.

festations associated with occult bleeding from a right-sided colonic tumour. Other presentations include intestinal obstruction (Fig. 12.4), perforation, prolapse of a rectal carcinoma at the anus (Fig. 12.5), or symptoms from metastases. Metastases are common in the liver and may occasionally appear calcified on a plain abdominal radiograph (Fig. 12.6). Any site may become involved, including the lungs and even the umbilicus. Rectal bleeding is perhaps the most useful symptom diagnostically; when fresh blood mixed with the stool occurs in an adult, it must always be considered to be due to a carcinoma of the colon until proved otherwise.

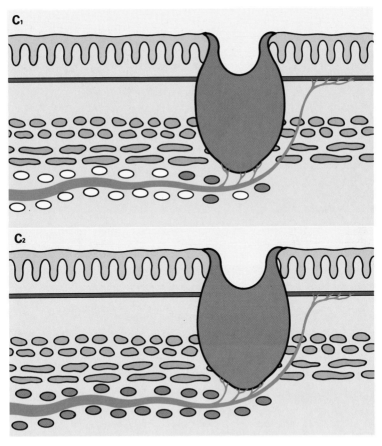

In C all layers are affected with the proximal lymph nodes affected in C1 and both the proximal and the highest resected nodes positive in C2.

Physical examination may show facial pallor because of blood loss from the colon or a mass palpable in the abdomen. A palpable nodular liver, multiple abdominal masses, jaundice and ascites are ominous signs which all suggest a late presentation of the disease. Digital examination of the rectum and sigmoidoscopy, with either a rigid or a flexible instrument, are essential in all patients with rectal bleeding or any other signs of colonic malignancy. A substantial number of neoplasms are within reach of the standard 25cm rigid sigmoidoscope and can be biopsied for histological confirmation of the diagnosis before surgery.

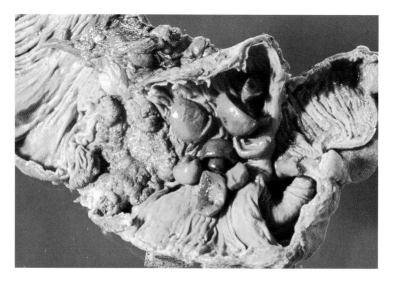

Fig. 12.4 Gross appearance of an obstructing carcinoma distal to the ileocaecal sphincter. Food (mushrooms) has accumulated proximal to the tumour.

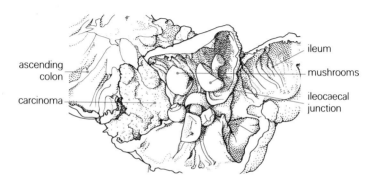

Most patients in whom colorectal cancer is suspected will need a barium enema for confirmation of the diagnosis and examination of the more proximal colon. The exceptions are patients with intestinal obstruction which fails to settle with conservative management and requires urgent surgery and those with histologically or cytologically diagnosed widespread metastases, unless surgical resection is contemplated to relieve obstructive symptoms.

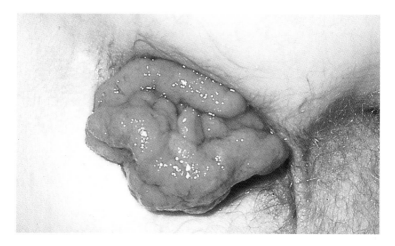

Fig. 12.5 A prolapsing rectal carcinoma. Courtesy of Mr. J.P.S. Thomson.

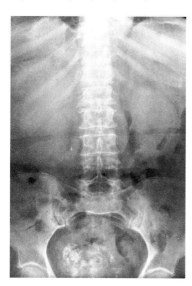

Fig. 12.6 Plain abdominal radiograph showing a calcified liver metastasis. There is gross hepatomegaly with faint microcalcification typical of a mucinous cystadenoma. The primary was a rectal carcinoma that had been resected. Local recurrence is demonstrated by the calcification in the pelvic cavity.

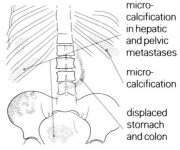

micro-calcification in hepatic and pelvic metastases

micro-calcification

displaced stomach and colon

A variety of appearances are seen on barium enema. Although an 'apple core' stricture is typical (Fig. 12.7), the lesion may be polypoid (Fig. 12.8) or plaque-like (Fig. 12.9). Usually these appearances taken in conjunction with the clinical features are diagnostic, and it

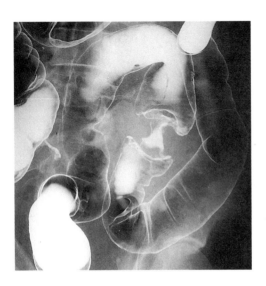

Fig. 12.7 Barium enema showing a typical annular carcinoma in the distal sigmoid.

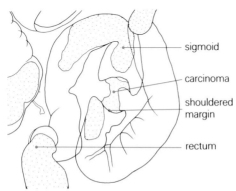

sigmoid

carcinoma

shouldered margin

rectum

is unnecessary to carry out further procedures before surgery. Occasionally, further investigation of a suspicious stricture, or a normal barium enema in a patient with an ominous clinical history, indicates colonoscopy. Certain areas of the colon are difficult to examine on

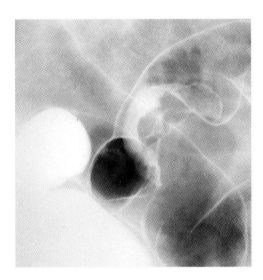

Fig. 12.8 Barium enema showing a large polypoid carcinoma in the sigmoid.

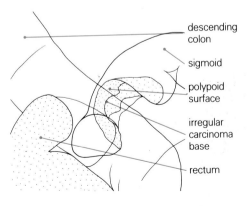

descending colon

sigmoid

polypoid surface

irregular carcinoma base

rectum

barium enema, particularly the sigmoid colon and caecum. Figure 12.10 shows the colonoscopic appearance of a neoplasm situated at the hepatic flexure which was missed on double-contrast barium enema.

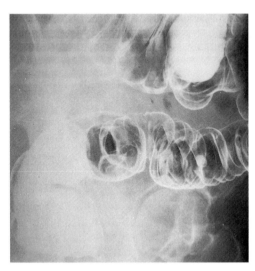

Fig. 12.9 Barium enema (oblique view) showing a plaque-like carcinoma in the sigmoid. The surface is only slightly irregular and the lesion is defined by its irregular elevated border, causing a haphazard line that crosses the normal mucosal lines where the thin barium layer coating the mucosa is seen tangentially.

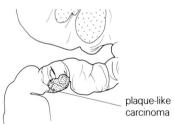

plaque-like carcinoma

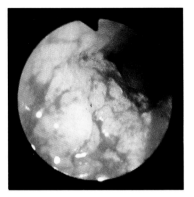

Fig. 12.10 Colonoscopic view of colonic cancer. Courtesy of Dr. C. Williams.

Most cancers of the colon and rectum are small, circumscribed and ulcerated with raised rolled edges (Fig. 12.11). Large fungating tumours are less common and predominate in the caecum (Fig. 12.12).

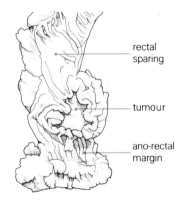

Fig. 12.11 Gross appearance of a carcinoma in the lower rectum; it is well circumscribed with raised edges and an ulcerated center.

rectal
sparing

tumour

ano-rectal
margin

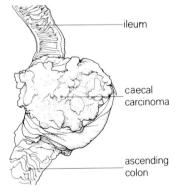

Fig. 12.12 Gross appearance of a large fungating carcinoma in the caecum.

ileum

caecal
carcinoma

ascending
colon

Annular stenosing tumours occur (12.13), but the diffusely infiltrating carcinoma akin to a gastric 'linitis plastica' is rare. A small proportion of tumours may appear mucoid. Over 80% of colorectal cancers seen histologically are adenocarcinomas of varying degrees of differentiation, similar to adenocarcinomas at other sites. Amongst the remaining patterns are mucinous adenocarcinomas, signet-ring

Fig. 12.13 Gross appearance of an annular stenosing carcinoma with proximal colonic dilatation.

annular tumour

proxima dilated colon

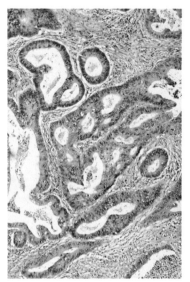

Fig. 12.14 Histological appearances of colonic cancer. In the moderately differentiated pattern, malignant epithelium forms obvious acini, but considerable nuclear pleomorphism remains within individual cells.

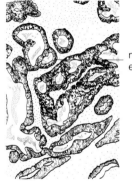

malignant epithelium

cancers, and undifferentiated and clear-cell varieties (Fig. 12.14). A careful examination of colorectal carcinomas will reveal residual adenoma in at least 15% of cases. This finding supports the theory that colorectal carcinomas develop by malignant transformation of adenomatous polyps.

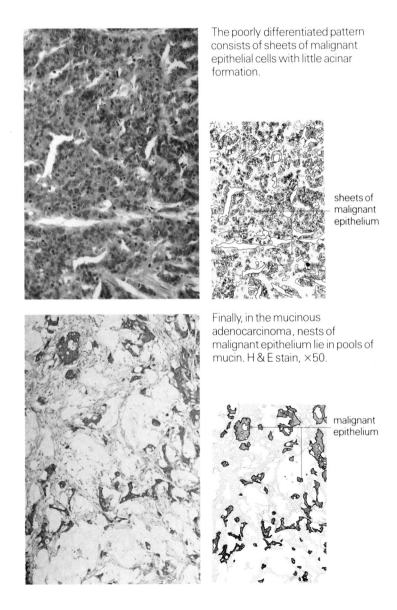

The poorly differentiated pattern consists of sheets of malignant epithelial cells with little acinar formation.

sheets of malignant epithelium

Finally, in the mucinous adenocarcinoma, nests of malignant epithelium lie in pools of mucin. H & E stain, ×50.

malignant epithelium

Polyps

Polyp is simply the descriptive term for any elevation of the intestinal surface. Colonic polyps are classified as neoplastic, hamartomatous, inflammatory and miscellaneous. They may be single or multiple (Fig. 12.15). The neoplastic or adenomatous variety is the most important group clinically, as it is considered to be premalignant.

Adenomatous Polyps

Adenomatous polyps may themselves give rise to symptoms, most commonly rectal bleeding or occasionally, if large enough, pain due to intussusception. Their importance relates to the potential of their epithelium to progress through varying degrees of dysplasia to carcinoma *in situ* and on to frankly invasive carcinoma. Approximately 75% of all colonic polyps are tubular adenomas, 15% are tubulovillous adenomas and 10% villous adenomas. The potential for malignant transformation is related to the morphology, size, degree of cellular atypia and number of polyps present. The presence of cancer in adenomas rises dramatically in polyps over 2cm in diameter. Thus, large multiple adenomas with a villous component are most likely to be malignant. Most colonic polyps are discovered either as an incidental

Classification of Polyps of the Large Intestine		
Type	**Single or Isolated**	**Polyposis**
Neoplastic	Tubular adenoma Tubulo-villous adenoma Villous adenoma	Familial adenomatous polyposis
Hamartomatous	Juvenile polyp	Juvenile polyposis
	Peutz-Jeghers polyp	Peutz-Jeghers syndrome
Inflammatory	Benign lymphoid polyp	Benign lymphoid polyposis
	Inflammatory 'pseudopolyp'	Inflammatory polyposis
Miscellaneous	Metaplastic (hyperplastic polyp) Lipoma, Neurofibroma, etc.	Metaplastic polyposis

Fig. 12.15 Classification of colonic polyps.

finding on a barium enema performed for unrelated symptoms or because of rectal bleeding (Figs. 12.16 and 12.17). Most polyps are asymptomatic and are therefore undetected during their early development. Once a polyp has become symptomatic, there is an increased likelihood that it has also become malignant.

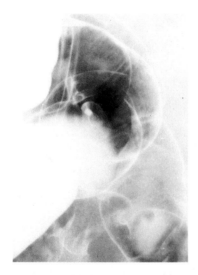

Fig. 12.16 Barium enema showing a pedunculated polyp en face (left). The two rings formed by the polyp and the stalk are called the 'target sign'

concentric rings due to head and stalk of polyp

The lateral decubitus view confirms that the polyp is pedunculated

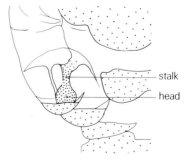

stalk

head

Following the demonstration of a polyp radiologically, it can be visualized and removed colonoscopically (Fig. 12.18). With an increased understanding of the adenoma-adenocarcinoma transformation, it is now believed that patients should undergo colonoscopy at routine intervals following the detection and removal of their original polyp or carcinoma. If any further polyps have developed they can be removed without the need for repeated radiological studies.

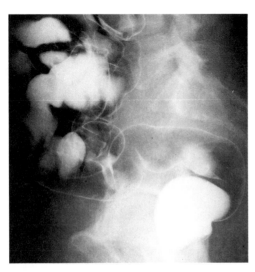

Fig. 12.17 Barium enema showing a small sessile polyp in the sigmoid. The coating over the top of the polyp and the meniscus around its base produces the 'hat' sign, which distinguishes small sessile polyps from other small ring shadows due to artefacts such as residue and air bubbles.

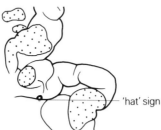

'hat' sign

The architecture of the dysplastic mucosa determines the appearance of the polyp, but a continuous macroscopic and microscopic spectrum exists from tubular adenomas, through tubulo-villous, to pure villous adenomas (Fig. 12.19).

The typical tubular adenoma is usually less than 1.5cm in diameter and pedunculated with a lobulated surface (Fig. 12.20). By contrast, the typical villous adenoma is large and sessile with a shaggy surface

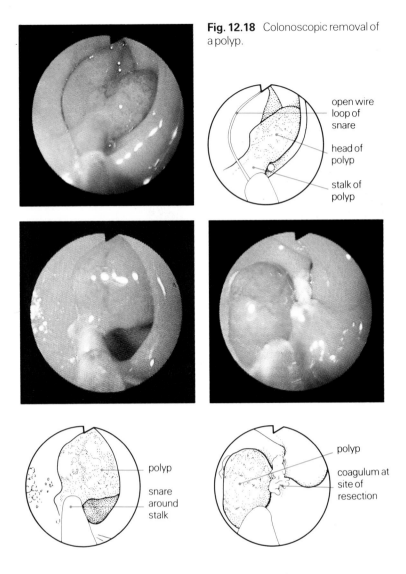

Fig. 12.18 Colonoscopic removal of a polyp.

open wire loop of snare

head of polyp

stalk of polyp

polyp

snare around stalk

polyp

coagulum at site of resection

Tubular

proliferating
tubules

stalk of
polyp

muscularis
mucosae

submucosa

muscularis
propria

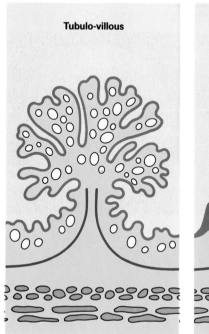

Fig. 12.19 Diagram showing the different patterns of colonic polyp.

Tubulo-villous

Villous

Fig. 12.20 Gross appearance of typical stalked and sessile tubular adenomas showing their lobulated surface. The large sessile adenoma contained a focus of carcinoma . A close-up view of a stalked adenoma is shown .

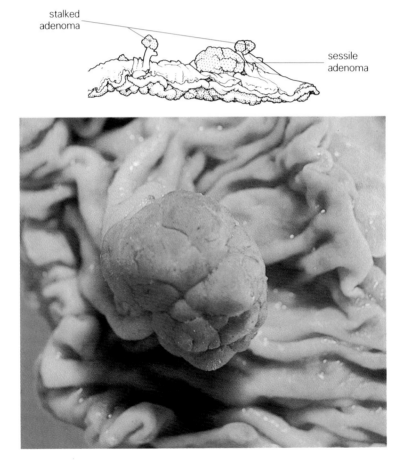

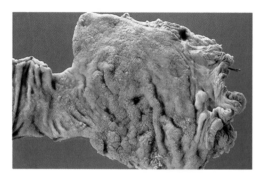

Fig. 12.21 Two typical macroscopic patterns of large villous adenomas. A finer villous pattern gives the mucosa a velvet appearance in contrast to the coarser pattern.

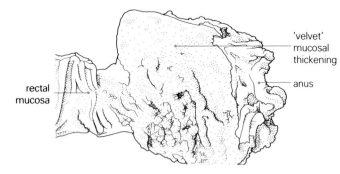

'velvet' mucosal thickening

anus

rectal mucosa

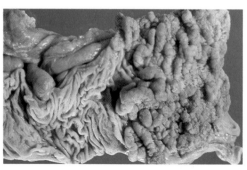

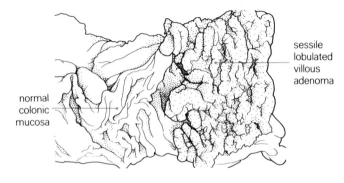

sessile lobulated villous adenoma

normal colonic mucosa

(Fig. 12.21). On microscopy the tubular and tubulovillous adenoma consists of closely-packed dysplastic epithelial tubules, separated by lamina propria. The stalk is composed of submucosa and normal mucosa (Fig. 12.22). The pure villous adenoma comprises large numbers of finger-like villi, with dysplastic epithelium over a core of lamina propria.

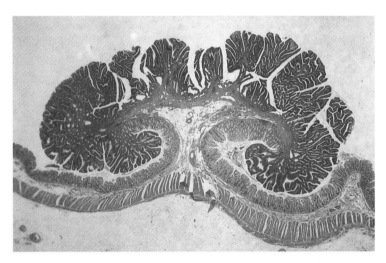

Fig. 12.22 Histological appearance of a typical stalked tubulo-villous adenoma. H & E stain, ×10.

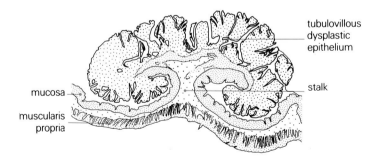

They rest directly on the muscularis mucosa (Fig. 12.23). The degree of cytological and architectural abnormality determines the severity of the dysplasia, and the severity of the dysplasia in turn determines the likelihood of malignant transformation (Fig. 12.24).

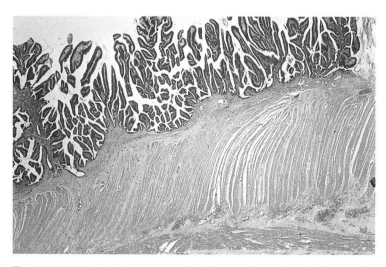

Fig. 12.23 Histological appearance of a villous papilloma showing its sessile nature. H & E stain, ×12.

dysplastic villous epithelium

muscularis mucosa and submucosa

muscularis propria

Early Colorectal Cancer (The Malignant Polyp)

Adenomas are benign and have no metastatic potential until dysplastic epithelium penetrates the muscularis mucosa and reaches the submucosa (Figs. 12.25 and 12.26). In this situation the term malignant

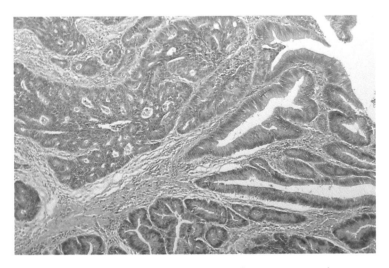

Fig. 12.24 The head of a tubular adenoma showing two patterns of dysplasia. At this magnification the architectural rather than the cytological differences are most apparent. H & E stain, ×75.

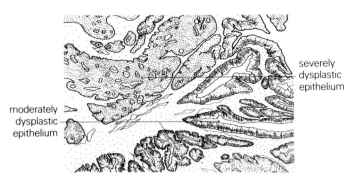

moderately dysplastic epithelium

severely dysplastic epithelium

polyp or early carcinoma is used. Provided that the base of the adenoma's stalk is free from invasion, there is no lymphatic penetration, and the carcinoma is not poorly differentiated. A local excision is believed to be sufficient therapy and outweighs the risks of major surgery.

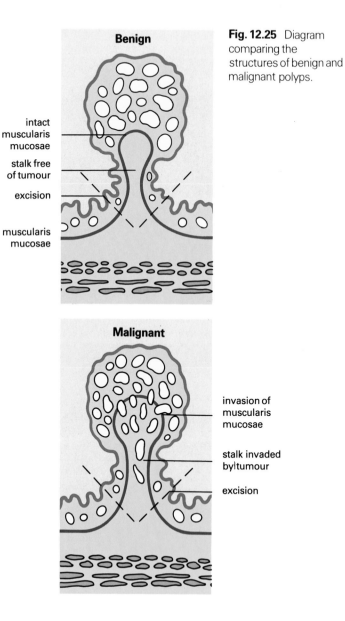

Fig. 12.25 Diagram comparing the structures of benign and malignant polyps.

Studies of the adenoma-carcinoma sequence and of metachronous cancer rates indicate that the cycle of change takes at least 3-5 years. This is taken into account when planning follow-up studies of patients for cancer prevention.

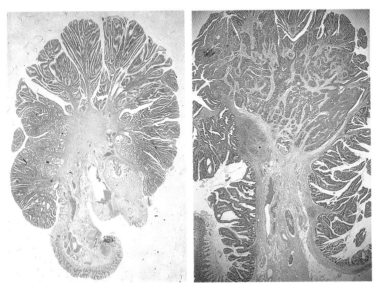

Fig. 12.26 Histological appearances demonstrating the difference between benign and malignant adenomatous lesions. In the benign case (left) the muscularis is intact, whereas in the malignant lesion (right), the muscularis mucosa is obviously invaded by malignant epithelium. Malignant glands in the lymphatics are seen close to the stalk of the base. H & E stain, ×8.

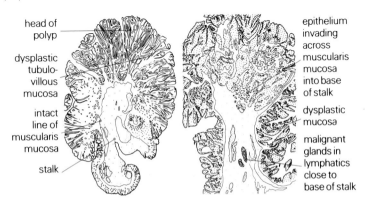

head of polyp

dysplastic tubulo-villous mucosa

intact line of muscularis mucosa

stalk

epithelium invading across muscularis mucosa into base of stalk

dysplastic mucosa

malignant glands in lymphatics close to base of stalk

The Non-Neoplastic Polyps

Miscellaneous

The most common non-neoplastic polyp is the metaplastic, or hyperplastic, polyp, which is most frequently found in the rectum but can occur anywhere in the colon. It is nearly always multiple and usually

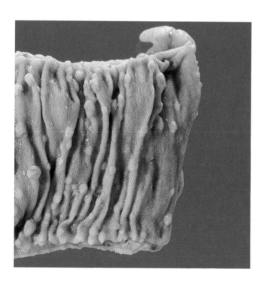

Fig. 12.27 A short length of colon covered with tiny sessile metaplastic polyps.

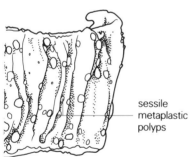

sessile metaplastic polyps

an incidental finding on radiological or endoscopic examination. Their numbers increase with age. Macroscopically, they appear as sessile mucosal elevations, rarely larger than 0.5cm in diameter (Fig. 12.27). Microscopically, they are elongated dilated tubules, the epithelium having a serrated pattern (Fig. 12.28).

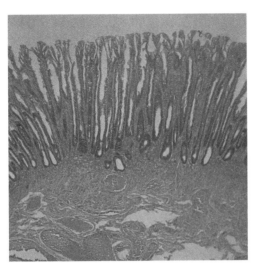

Fig. 12.28 Histological appearance of a metaplastic polyp showing its sessile nature and the dilated crypts, which have a serrated appearance due to the uneven height of the lining cells. H & E stain, ×20.

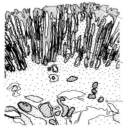

serrated cryptal epithelium

elongated dilated crypts

muscularis mucosa

Inflammatory

This group includes benign lymphoid polyps and the inflammatory 'pseudo-polyps' seen in chronic inflammatory bowel disease.

Lymphoid polyps are most common in the rectum, usually appear without symptoms and measure up to 2-3cms. They comprise normal lymphoid tissue with a prominent follicular pattern (Fig. 12.29).

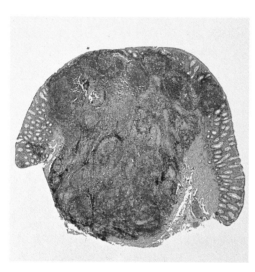

Fig. 12.29 A section across a typical lymphoid polyp removed from the rectum. H & E stain, ×10.

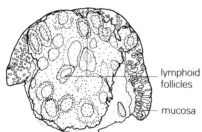

lymphoid follicles

mucosa

Inflammatory pseudopolyps are the result of defective mucosal healing following a bout of severe ulceration (Fig. 12.30). They comprise granulation tissue and/or branched tags of mucosa (Fig. 12.31). They are usually multiple and easily mistaken for adenomas in barium studies and at colonoscopy.

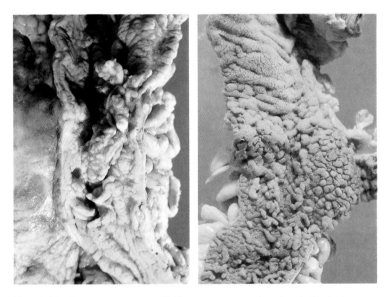

Fig. 12.30 Gross appearance of inflammatory pseudopolyps in Crohn's colitis (left) and ulcerative colitis (right).

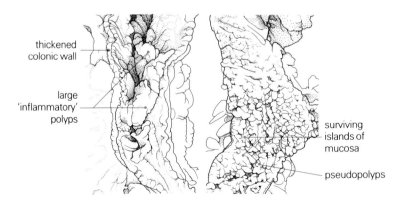

thickened colonic wall

large 'inflammatory' polyps

surviving islands of mucosa

pseudopolyps

Hamartomas

The hamartomatous polyps comprise the juvenile polyp and the polyp of the Peutz-Jeghers syndrome.

Juvenile polyps occur most often in the rectum in the young, but occasionally in adults. They are smooth and round, and the cut surface is frequently cystic. On microscopy they appear as dilated epithelial tubules sited in abundant stroma (Fig. 12.32). They have a similar structure to some inflammatory polyps. There is no stalk, and it is

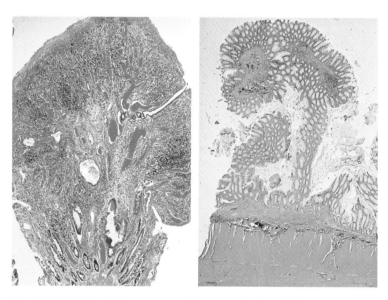

Fig. 12.31 Histological appearance of the two varieties of inflammatory pseudopolyp: a polyp comprising granulation tissue (left, ×50) and polypoid tags of vitually normal mucosa (right, ×8). H & E stain.

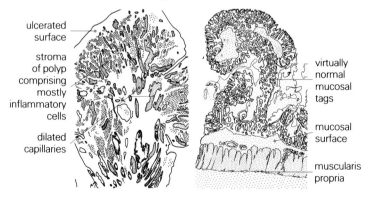

ulcerated surface

stroma of polyp comprising mostly inflammatory cells

dilated capillaries

virtually normal mucosal tags

mucosal surface

muscularis propria

common for these polyps to auto-amputate. The Peutz-Jeghers polyp (Fig. 12.33) is part of the Peutz-Jeghers syndrome. This is an autosomal dominant condition comprising circumoral and cutaneous pigmentation with hamartomatous polyps at varying sites in the gastro-intestinal tract, most commonly in the small intestine. The striking histological feature is the arborization of the muscularis mucosa around the branched epithelial tubules within the lamina propria (Fig. 12.34).

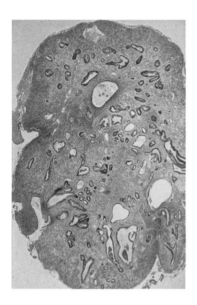

Fig. 12.32 Histological appearance of a juvenile polyp showing the abundant stromal element and the cystic glands. H & E stain, ×8.

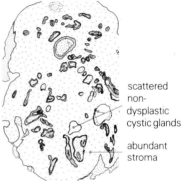

scattered non-dysplastic cystic glands

abundant stroma

Fig. 12.33 A Peutz-Jeghers polyp in the ileum which had intussuscepted through the ileocaecal sphincter into the colon. Courtesy of Dr. J. Newman.

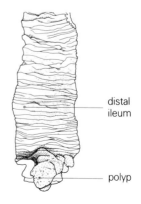

distal ileum

polyp

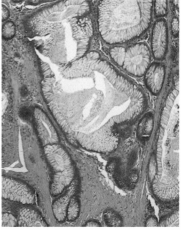

Fig. 12.34 Histological appearance of a Peutz-Jeghers polyp. At low power (left, ×12) the characteristic intermingling of glands and muscularis is seen. At high power (right, ×50) the features are more obvious. There is no dysplastic element. H & E stain.

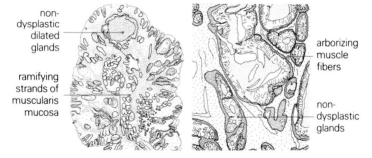

non-dysplastic dilated glands

ramifying strands of muscularis mucosa

arborizing muscle fibers

non-dysplastic glands

Familial Polyposis Syndromes	
Associated with a high risk of malignancy	**Not associated with a high risk of malignancy**
Familial adenomatous colonic polyposis	Peutz-Jeghers syndrome
Generalized adenomatous polyposis	Juvenile polyposis coli
Gardner's syndrome	Generalized gastrointestinal juvenile polyposis
Turcot-Depre's syndrome	Cronkhite-Canada syndrome

Fig. 12.35 Table of familial polyposis syndromes.

Multiple Polyposis Syndromes

The inherited polyposis syndromes (Fig. 12.35) account for only a small proportion of gastrointestinal polyps. Nevertheless, their importance lies in the risk of malignant transformation at a young age. In those disorders with adenomatous polyps (Fig. 12.36), there is a marked possibility of preventing this by elective colectomy. The syndromes associated with a high risk of gastrointestinal carcinoma include familial polyposis, which can involve changes along the entire gastrointestinal

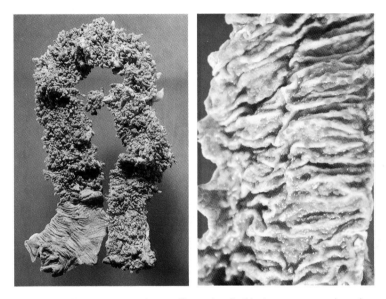

Fig. 12.36 Colectomy specimens illustrating florid adenomatous polyposis. The larger size and stalked nature of the polyps in the specimen on the left contrast with those in the specimen on the right which are tiny and sessile.

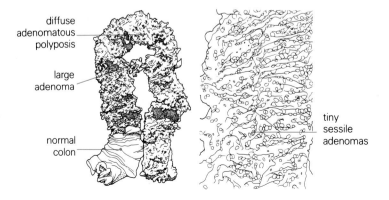

diffuse adenomatous polyposis

large adenoma

normal colon

tiny sessile adenomas

tract, Gardner's syndrome, which is adenomatous polyposis coli associated with osteomas and soft tissue tumours (Fig. 12.37), and Turcot-Depre's syndrome, which is a similar syndrome associated with tumours of the central nervous system. All of these conditions are inherited as an autosomal dominant (Fig. 12.38) and have a malignant potential which, in the case of familial polyposis and Gardner's syndrome, may be greater than 95%.

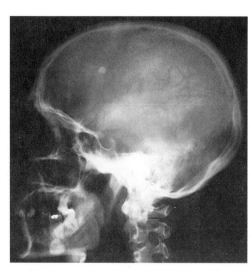

Fig. 12.37 Skull radiograph in Gardner's syndrome showing osteoma in the skull vault and two further lesions in the mandible.

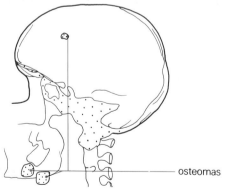

osteomas

Other inherited multiple polyposis syndromes occur which are associated with an increased incidence of carcinoma, although the risk is not high. Their common feature is that the polyps are not adenomatous. The most frequent of these conditions is Peutz-Jeghers syndrome which is of dominant inheritance and in which there is a low yet definite risk of gastrointestinal cancer. This may reflect a predisposition for dysplasia in the epithelium covering the hamartomatous polyps, which

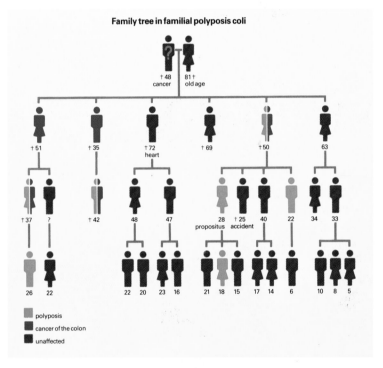

Fig. 12.38 Family tree in familial polyposis coli. The general picture is that of a Mendelian characteristic, in which the child of an affected parent has a 50-50 chance of inheriting the condition and where children not inheriting the defective gene cannot pass it on to any of their dependents. Courtesy of Dr. H.J.R. Busey.

are not themselves malignant. The extra-intestinal manifestations of Peutz-Jeghers syndrome have been described above: figure 12.39 illustrates the circumoral pigmentation. The Cronkhite-Canada syndrome includes alopecia, hyperpigmentation, and onychodystrophy (Fig. 12.40). The polyps have some resemblance to the juvenile variety with large cystic glands being the major element (Fig. 12.41).

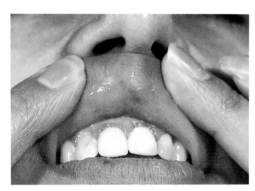

Fig. 12.39 The lips in Peutz-Jeghers syndrome showing the blue macules.

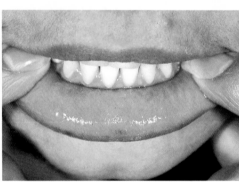

The most important information required for the differential diagnosis of the polyposis syndromes includes the number and distribution of polyps within the gut, their histological appearance and the nature and extent of any extra-intestinal manifestations. Barium enema and sigmoidoscopy are necessary in these patients and may reveal literally hundreds of polyps (Figs. 12.42 and 12.43). If the

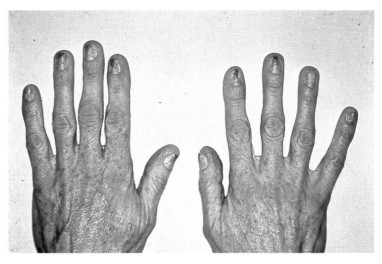

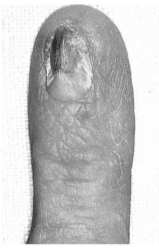

Fig. 12.40 Onychodystrophy in the Cronkhite-Canada syndrome. Courtesy of Dr. W.J. Cunliffe.

condition does not carry a high risk of malignancy, repeated colonoscopic removal of the larger polyps may suffice. However, patients with those syndromes which have a risk of malignancy approaching 100% require prophylactic colectomy.

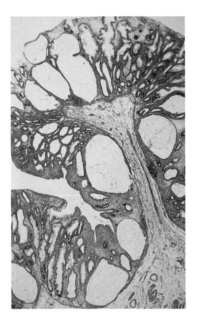

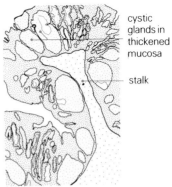

Fig. 12.41 Histological appearance in the Cronkhite-Canada syndrome. The cystic glands are neither dysplastic nor accompanied by a stromal element. These features differentiate them from other forms. H & E stain, ×8.

cystic glands in thickened mucosa

stalk

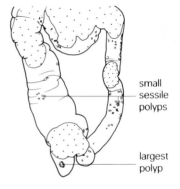

Fig. 12.42 Barium enema showing polyps throughout the colon and rectum. Most are sessile and measure less than 1cm across, though the largest polyps found in the rectum measure 1.5cm.

small sessile polyps

largest polyp

The histological appearance of these tumours varies, although all those with a high potential for malignancy are invariably adenomatous. They correspond exactly with the patterns seen in the individual varieties.

Volvulus

A volvulus occurs when a portion of the alimentary tract rotates or twists about itself. In the colon this usually involves either the caecum or the sigmoid. A caecal volvulus occurs between a mobile caecum and ascending colon, a congenital anomaly which may in turn be associated with malrotation and incomplete descent of the caecum. A sigmoid volvulus is particularly likely to occur when the mesentery is unduly long and has a narrow attachment, or when the sigmoid colon itself is abnormally long. Although a sigmoid volvulus is uncommon in Western populations, its frequency is higher in populations with a very high intake of dietary fibre; this is probably associated with a long sigmoid colon and faecal loading. Although any age group may be affected, most patients with a sigmoid volvulus are elderly.

Patients with a caecal and a sigmoid volvulus present with large bowel obstruction which may be either acute, recurrent or chronic. A plain radiograph of the abdomen is usually either diagnostic or highly suggestive (Fig. 12.44). Sigmoid volvulus can often be reduced by passing of a flatus tube, or a colonoscope, but these procedures are not as effective with a caecal volvulus. When such conservative measures fail, or when the arterial supply to the gut has been compromised, laparotomy and surgical reduction of the volvulus are necessary (Fig. 12.45). Following reduction, the caecum or sigmoid is usually fixed in order to prevent a recurrence.

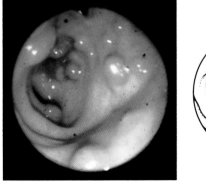

Fig. 12.43 Colonoscopic appearance in polyposis coli. Courtesy of Dr. C. Williams.

Vascular Malformations

The most common vascular malformation of the colon is angiodysplasia. This is a well defined, clinical and pathological entity characteristically involving the caecum and ascending colon and usually affecting patients in their seventh and eighth decades. Angiodysplasia is occasionally associated with aortic stenosis or chronic obstructive airways disease and, in these situations, may occur in a younger age group. The lesions are usually small and flat, and, as they are not revealed on barium enema, their identification was elusive for many years. Colonoscopy has shown that the areas of vascular abnormality are a common cause of episodic, usually low grade, colonic bleeding in elderly patients. At colonoscopy the lesions are usually seen to lie in the right colon and appear bright red (Fig. 12.46).

In the acutely bleeding patient in whom colonoscopy may be difficult, selective angiography can occasionally show areas of ectatic vasculature, but frequently the lesions are too small to be detected. A useful radiological clue is the rapid and early filling of the draining vein (Fig. 12.47). Figure 12.48 shows areas of angiodysplasia in a gross specimen following right hemicolectomy for recurrent lower gastro-

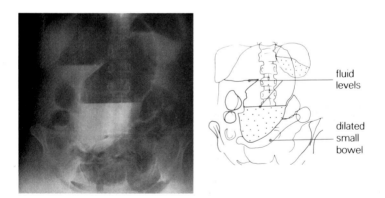

Fig. 12.44 Erect abdominal radiograph in a case of caecal volvulus. There are two large fluid levels in a distended loop of bowel having a 'coffee bean' shape, with some gaseous distension in the small bowel. The hilum of the distended loop is formed by the twisted mesentery and points to the right iliac fossa. The presence of proximal small bowel obstruction confirms a caecal volvulus.

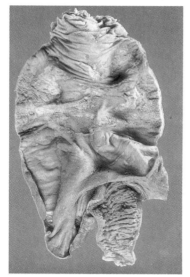
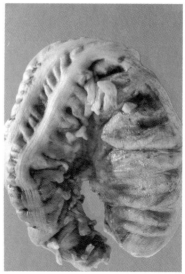

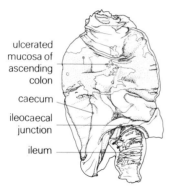

ulcerated
mucosa of
ascending
colon

caecum

ileocaecal
junction

ileum

Fig. 12.45 An opened right hemicolectomy from a caecal volvulus (left) and an unopened resection of a sigmoid volvulus (right).

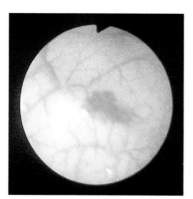

Fig. 12.46 Colonoscopic appearance in angiodysplasia. Courtesy of Dr. C. Williams.

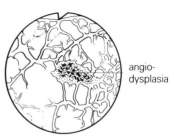

angio-
dysplasia

intestinal bleeding. Histologically, a spectrum of changes may be present, from a small number of dilated submucosal veins, with only a few thin-walled capillaries in the mucosa, to an obvious cluster of vessels communicating with ectatic capillaries, which replaces an area

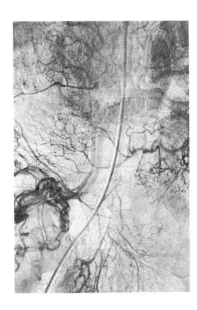

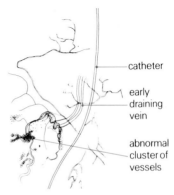

Fig. 12.47 Superior mesenteric angiogram (subtraction film), late arteriolar phase showing an abnormal cluster of vessels in the caecum, typical of angiodysplasia. Courtesy of Prof. D. Allison.

catheter

early draining vein

abnormal cluster of vessels

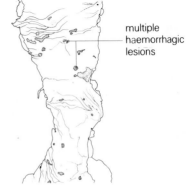

Fig. 12.48 A length of ascending colon in a right hemicolectomy showing multiple and angiodysplastic lesions in the mucosa.

multiple haemorrhagic lesions

of mucosa (Fig. 12.49). Arterial injection of barium sulphate into the freshly excised surgical specimen is the best method of finding small lesions that may not be apparent once the segment of colon has been enclosed (Fig. 12.50).

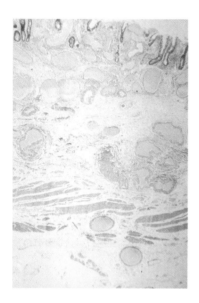

Fig. 12.49 The typical histological appearance of angiodysplasia showing the cluster of mucosal and submucosal vessels. They contain barium following the injection of the surgical specimen. H & E stain, ×20.

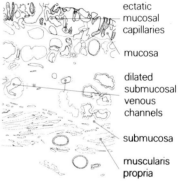

ectatic mucosal capillaries

mucosa

dilated submucosal venous channels

submucosa

muscularis propria

Fig. 12.50 Part of a right hemicolectomy after injection of barium sulphate into the fresh specimen, demonstrating a tiny angiodysplastic lesion.

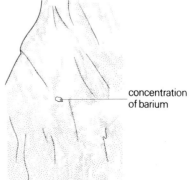

concentration of barium

INDEX

Note: the numbers in **bold** refer to Fig. numbers.